EXPERIENCE, INC.

MEN AND WOMEN WHO FOUNDED FAMOUS COMPANIES AFTER THE AGE OF 40

Joseph J. Fucini
Suzy Fucini

THE FREE PRESS
A Division of Macmillan, Inc.
NEW YORK

Collier Macmillan Publishers
LONDON

The Free Press
A Division of Macmillan, Inc.
866 Third Avenue, New York, N.Y. 10022

Collier Macmillan Canada, Inc.

Printed in the United States of America

printing number

1 2 3 4 5 6 7 8 9 10

Library of Congress Cataloging-in-Publication Data

Fucini, Joseph J.
  Experience, Inc.

  Bibliography: p.
  Includes index.
  1. Businessmen—Biography. 2. Entrepreneur—Biography.
I. Fucini, Suzy.   II. Title.
HC29.F834   1987   338′.04′0922 [B]   87–11984
ISBN 0-02-910971-X

We wish to acknowledge the following companies and individuals for permission to include the photographs used in this book: Joseph S. Tushinsky, Chatsworth, CA (1); TCBY Enterprises, Inc., Little Rock, AR (2); The Wiffle Ball Inc., Shelton, CT (3, 4); TII Industries, Inc., Toa Alta, PR (5); Bandag, Inc., Muscatine, IA (6); Isaac L. Eskenasy, Sarasota, FL (7); Winnebago Industries, Inc., Forest City, IA (8, 9); Tofutti Brands Inc., Rahway, NJ (10); Kinder-Care Learning Centers, Inc., Montgomery, AL (11); Home Shopping Network, Inc., Clearwater, FL (12); Businessland, Inc., San Jose, CA (14); Control Data Corp., Minneapolis, MN (13, 15); Seven Oaks International, Inc., Memphis, TN (16, 17); Willis K. Drake, Minneapolis, MN (18); W. L. Gore & Associates, Inc., Newark, DE (19); Ed H. Price, Bradenton, FL (20, 22, 23); Pentair, Inc., St. Paul, MN (21); Ugly Duckling Rent-A-Car System Inc., Tucson, AZ (25); Ramada Inns, Inc., Phoenix, AZ (24, 26, 27); Loctite Corp., Newington, CT (28, 29); David Lindsey, Plumly Industries, Inc., Fort Worth, TX (30).

Contents

iii

Acknowledgments

This book would not have been possible without the unselfish cooperation of many people. Foremost among them are the entrepreneurs themselves, who took time from busy schedules to participate in this project. Regrettably, not all the entrepreneurs we interviewed could be included in this book, and to those whose stories were omitted we extend our apologies along with our gratitude.

We would also like to thank the families, friends, and associates of our subjects. Their impressions and reminiscences were invaluable in the preparation of this book. Spatial limitations prohibit us from listing all these generous people by name, but we would be remiss if we did not acknowledge the very special help provided by Lucy Diana, Ike Eskenasy, David Lindsey, David A. Mullany, Jr., Ann Muscari, Ed H. Price, Jr., Robert A. Schneider, and Leon Shimkin.

Our work as researchers was made much easier by the skilled and courteous staffs of the Ann Arbor (Michigan) Public Library, the New York Public Library, the University of Michigan Business School Library, and the University of Michigan Graduate School Library. The New York and Philadelphia offices of Right Associates, one of the nation's leading outplacement agencies, provided us with valuable insight into the unique problems and concerns faced by older entrepreneurs.

We are indebted to Robert Wallace and Karen Ott of The Free Press for their wise and well-timed encouragement and suggestions. Finally, we would like to extend our special thanks to Meghan Robinson Wander, whose friendship and forbearance never let us down.

Preface

Between 1987 and 2000, nearly 55 million Americans will celebrate their fortieth birthdays.[1] In so doing, they will pass a milestone that is typically associated with a greater degree of self-evaluation than any other time of life.

Forty is the halfway point between 20 and 60, the midway mark between the beginning of adulthood and the dawning of old age. It is a time when people instinctively ask themselves if they are truly happy with their lives and accomplishments; a time to consider making changes, fueled by a now-or-never feeling that psychologists have labeled, and the media has sensationalized, as "mid-life crisis."

For many, this crisis will revolve around a single question: "Am I happy with my career?" The middle-aged executive employed at an unfulfilling job will often experience an urge to strike out on his or her own, to give up the security of a corporate position for the chance of winning greater rewards—both financial and emotional—as an entrepreneur.

There are many reasons why the approach of middle age galvanizes the would-be entrepreneur into action. Some view their forties as the last chance to act on a long-cherished idea for a product, service, or other business. Other mature executives choose to go the entrepreneurial route after finding the path to further advancement or promotion blocked at their current positions.

In recent years, another more pressing catalyst has been added to these common motives for mid-life entrepreneurship. The wave of corporate mergers that began in the 1970s, and gained momentum in the 1980s, has resulted in an epidemic of white-collar layoffs. Corporations seeking to trim redundant middle- and upper-level management positions have let go record numbers of high-salaried executives by either dismissing them outright or offering early-retirement incentives. These terminated executives often have a difficult time finding new jobs that offer a salary commensurate with their skill and experience. Faced with this situation, more and more of them are turning to entrepreneurship as an alternative to re-employment.

The growing trend toward entrepreneurship among America's rapidly graying population raises important questions about the role of age in business start-ups. Does the mid-life entrepreneur face special problems not shared by his or her younger counterpart? Does the entrepreneur's age influence the way potential investors view his or her proposed venture? Does it affect the way he or she plans and manages the new business? Is being over 40 an asset or a liability for the entrepreneur?

We have sought answers to these questions by looking into the lives and careers of men and women who, at mid-life, started such famous companies as Ramada Inns, Diners Club, Winnebago, and Tropicana Orange Juice. During the course of our research, we studied nearly one hundred post-40 entrepreneurs and finally selected twenty-nine for inclusion in this book. Although the chosen twenty-nine all enjoyed an extraordinary degree of financial success, the factors that inspired them, and the challenges they encountered, are typical of all mid-life entrepreneurs. Thus, we believed that an examination of their careers would shed valuable light on our age/entrepreneurship questions.

We have organized our profiles of these entrepreneurs into seven thematic sections, each containing from three to five biographical sketches. The section themes are based on the pivotal factors that prompted the entrepreneurs to start their post-40 businesses.

In the "Drawing Ace" section, we include the stories of individuals who became so enthused about a particular product they had created or discovered that they decided to use it as the basis of a post-40 business.

The "Upping the Stakes" section contains accounts of entrepreneurs who already owned moderately successful businesses, but whose growing ambition led them to risk their security for a new, and potentially more lucrative, venture.

"Riding a Wave" features entrepreneurs who recognized a significant societal or consumer trend in its earliest stages and took advantage of the opportunity to jump on the bandwagon with a product or service.

"Plugging a Gap" is devoted to individuals who spotted an unfilled need in the marketplace or a weakness in an established company's marketing strategy and stepped in to fill this void.

"Jumping the Fence" profiles entrepreneurs who developed a concept for a product while working at another company and, after having the idea vetoed by their employer, went off to pursue it on their own.

"Making It Happen" tells the stories of individuals who *first* determined they wanted to be in business for themselves and *then* cast about for a suitable product or service on which to build a company; the nature of their enterprise was very secondary to their desire to be in the driver's seat.

Finally, "Building a Nest" profiles individuals whose primary motivation in starting a post-40 business was to ensure themselves financial security or a productive life during their retirement years.

We established two essential criteria that had to be met for subjects to be included in this book: first, the individual had to have founded a successful company at the age of 40 or older; and second, the new business had to represent a significant step upward for the entrepreneur in terms of income, power, and/or prestige.

Unfortunately, spatial limitations forced us to omit the stories of many individuals who engineered impressive entrepreneurial feats at mid-life. Two of America's best-known post-40 entrepreneurs, Ray Kroc and Colonel Harland Sanders, were not included in this book because their stories have been told often and well in the past and little would be accomplished by repeating them in these pages.

In addition to our desire to give recognition to some deserving lesser-known entrepreneurs, we wanted to present a mix of subjects that would provide a well-balanced cross-section of industries, products, and services. Another factor taken into account was the subject's relevance to the contemporary business scene. Most of the companies featured in this book were started after 1960; those which date farther back were included chiefly because their founders pioneered new products or services that had a significant and enduring impact on the marketplace.

One requirement we did not have was that our subjects maintain an unbroken record of success after founding their companies. Although all the individuals whose careers are described in this book benfited financially from their entrepreneurial endeavors, not all their stories had unqualified happy endings.

Entrepreneurs are by nature risk takers; they are often at odds temperamentally with the corporate administrators who, in a typical scenario, are brought in to manage a company once it has grown beyond the initial stages. As the corporate cycle progresses, it is not uncommon for conflicts to develop between the founder, who may wish to continue pursuing high-risk ventures, and a management team inclined to steer the firm in a more conservative direction. This gulf may widen to the point where the entrepreneur is eventually relegated to a backseat role or forced out of his or her company altogether.

One of our subjects, ComputerLand founder William Millard, inadvertently planted the seeds of his own destruction when, in his overzealousness to acquire funding, he entered into an unwise agreement with a Massachusetts venture capital firm that later led to a lawsuit, costing him a 20 percent share of his privately held company and stripping him of its chairmanship.

At other times, when a strong-willed entrepreneur manages to maintain an autocratic grip on the reins of power and does not heed the advice of professional managers, the outcome can be equally catastrophic. Control Data Corp. founder and longtime chairman William Norris poured hundreds of millions of dollars into social programs that many executives and shareholders felt were not in the best interests of the company. It was only after the computer manufacturer suffered a loss of over a half billion dollars in 1985 that Norris was finally forced to step down.

We have included problematic stories of entrepreneurs like Norris and Millard to show some of the things that can—and frequently do—go awry in start-up ventures. Risks are as inherent to entrepreneurship as rewards, and, inevitably, some who take the risk will not fare as well as others. As authors, we felt it was our obligation to put this risk factor into perspective by de-voting a portion of our space to the less-than-desirable outcomes of certain entrepreneurial endeavors.

Despite the fact that some of our subjects ended up losing control of the companies they founded, it is our contention that they should not be regarded as failures. Indeed, all were suc-cessful vis-à-vis the goal they set out to accomplish: to build a profitable corporation from the ground up. And for all of them, the intrinsic satisfaction of molding an idea into a corporate real-ity was by far the greatest reward—more so than any long-term tenure as board chairperson or any financial remuneration, no matter how great. We believe that 77-year-old George Plumly of Plumly Industries summed up the sentiment of all our subjects when he said, "Business is a game to me. I do it because it's fun. The money is very secondary."

Introduction: Age Assets

What are the chances of a mid-life entrepreneur succeeding in a business of his or her own? Unfortunately, the odds of any new enterprise surviving, no less prospering, are slim, regardless of the age of its founder. According to Dun & Bradstreet, nearly four out of ten businesses fail before celebrating their third anniversary.[1] This figure increases to six out of ten after 5 years and eight out of ten after a decade.

Although there are no statistics specifically related to the failure rates of businesses founded by men and women over 40, it is generally assumed that these individuals, by getting a late start, have simply added yet another obstacle to the peril-wrought path of entrepreneurship. Indeed, in our traditionally youth-oriented culture, age typically has been viewed as an impediment to entrepreneurial success. Some skeptics have questioned whether post-40 entrepreneurs possess the stamina and energy required to get a new business off the ground, or whether they are too set in their ways to respond to the changes that inevitably occur in any market situation.

After studying the lives of the twenty-nine individuals in this book, we have come to the conclusion that these concerns are completely and utterly unfounded. Far from being a liability, age actually facilitated the successfulness of these entrepreneurs, endowing them with a variety of advantages that we call "age assets."

Age assets fall into two broad categories: internal and external. Internal age assets are personality traits such as confidence, resourcefulness, and resiliency that are developed and strengthened through experience. External age assets are circumstantial advantages that accrue over the course of a career, such as a respected professional reputation, financial freedom, and an "insider's" position that alerts one to new trends and opportunities as they develop in a particular industry.

We have identified eight general age assets shared by all or most of the entrepreneurs in this book:

- *Confidence.* A track record of successful accomplishments as a corporate employee will help an individual develop the self-confidence needed to strike out on his or her own. Such was the case with John Psarouthakis, a 46-year-old engineer who started the $234 million J. P. Industries in 1978, after having spent most of his career working for large corporations. Prior to launching his company, Psarouthakis was a group vice-president at the Detroit conglomerate Masco Corp., where he was responsible for improving the efficiency of underperforming manufacturing acquisitions. His ability as a corporate troubleshooter played a key role in the company's phenomenal growth during the 1970s, a decade that saw Masco's sales jump from $69.4 million to $726.4 million. Encouraged by this success, Psarouthakis started his own company, J. P. Industries, a mini-conglomerate that duplicated the Masco formula, acquiring anemic plumbing and transportation supply manufacturers and restoring them to profitability.

- *Objectivity.* Although entrepreneurs over 40 tend to exhibit greater confidence in their abilities, they are, at the same time, more prone to have a realistic view of their limitations. Because of this objectivity, the older entrepreneur is more likely to seek outside advice or to team up with others whose professional backgrounds complement his or her own. Back in 1939, when Robert de Graff hit upon the idea for the first mass-market paperback book, he drew up plans to start Pocket Books, Inc. However, realizing that he knew very little about corporate management, the 45-year-old entrepreneur wisely took on three publishing veterans as partners—Richard Simon, Max Schuster, and Leon Shimkin—all from Simon & Schuster. The trio's experience in running a publishing company helped Pocket Books become an immediate success.

- *Resourcefulness.* After having spent 20 or 30 years out in the work world, the older entrepreneur has acquired a "street smart" sense of business. He can reach into his repertoire of experiences and pull out innovative solutions to the financing, production, and marketing problems that arise in the course of a new business start-up. Perry Mendel, a former shopping center developer who founded Kinder-Care Learning Centers, Inc., drew upon his intimate knowledge of real estate financing to raise money for the rapid expansion of his child care company. Mendel lacked the capital needed to build a nationwide chain of child care centers in the early 1970s. He could have expanded through franchising, but doing so would have made it difficult to maintain control over the level of Kinder-Care's service. Instead, Mendel turned to a plan he had once used to finance the construction of shopping centers: he solicited investors in cities throughout the U.S. to put up $150,000 each to construct new Kinder-Care centers, and agreed in turn to lease the buildings from these investors for a 30-year period. With a ready source of capital thus guaranteed, Mendel was able to expand his Kinder-Care chain to 335 centers, netting annual earnings of $2.2 million by 1980.
- *Resiliency.* By the time he or she has reached mid-life, the average person has traveled through the peaks and valleys that mark most career paths. This gives the entrepreneur an overview that makes it possible to see beyond temporary setbacks, leaving him or her better equipped to bounce back from any reversals encountered when starting a business. Because of this resiliency, the older entrepreneur is often able to turn a mistake into a learning experience. A case in point is 55-year-old Jacob Barowsky, the creator of Lestoil household cleaner. When Barowsky introduced Lestoil to the New England market after World War II, the product died on supermarket shelves despite the fact that it was being promoted by an extensive newspaper, radio, and TV campaign. The problem, Barowsky eventually realized, was that the ads were being spread too thinly, over too many different media in too many cities, to make a strong impact on consumers. His solution was to sink all his ad dollars into one medium— television—and to concentrate on breaking Lestoil into a single market at a time. Barowsky ran a TV blitz for Lestoil in Holyoke, Massachusetts, followed by campaigns in Springfield and New Haven. Within four years, Lestoil's sales had increased by 44,000

percent, and the product was being sold in supermarkets throughout the East and Midwest.

• *Commitment.* The would-be entrepreneur with years of business experience behind him or her is better able to define precise goals for a new company and make realistic projections about the time, effort, and capital required to achieve success. Because they are more realistic in assessing the challenges before them, mature entrepreneurs tend to approach their new businesses with a deeper sense of commitment than their more naive under-40 counterparts. A number of our subjects, including Wilbert Gore (W. L. Gore & Associates) and Murray Harpole (Pentair, Inc.), told us that when starting their businesses, they made a firm commitment to stick it out for a predetermined amount of time (Gore for two years and Harpole for five years). By establishing such time-frames, these entrepreneurs effectively cut off the psychological option of quitting during the commitment period. This allowed them to concentrate more intently on achieving their business goals free from the distraction of self-doubt or second-guessing.

• *Reputation.* The reputation that an entrepreneur has developed in a business or profession is a valuable asset in attracting investors and key employees. With longer career histories behind them, older entrepreneurs have had more opportunities to build strong professional reputations than individuals under 40. William Norris traded on the reputation he had developed as an executive at two pioneering computer firms, Engineering Research Associates and Sperry's UNIVAC division, to raise start-up capital for his own high-tech company, Control Data Corp., in 1957. In what was one of the earliest experiments in venture capital financing, the 45-year-old Norris was able to sell 1.4 million one-dollar shares in Control Data to outside investors. People bought the shares even though the proposed company had no employees, no facility, and no product at the time—only the reputation of a founder who had twice proven his genius in the computer industry.

• *Freedom.* The middle and retirement years often bring about a measure of freedom from financial worries, career commitments, and child-rearing responsibilities. This affords the individual the luxury of gambling time and money on a new business venture. Ramada Inns, Inc. was started by a 50-year-old

4

Arizona retiree, Marion W. Isbell, whose previous involvement in the restaurant business had made him a millionaire. Another retiree, 55-year-old engineer Carl G. Sontheimer, found himself with more time to devote to his culinary hobby in 1969. After dabbling briefly as a cooking teacher and a food writer, Sontheimer launched a cookware importing business that ultimately grew into the food processor company Cuisinart, Inc.

- *Insider's Knowledge.* A would-be entrepreneur who has been involved in a particular industry for a number of years tends to become intimately familiar with its inner workings. This insider's perspective often allows one to recognize emerging trends and opportunities before they become known to those outside the industry. Some entrepreneurs, such as Sam Sarno, have used this knowledge to start a successful post-40 business. A Memphis, Tennessee, grocer, Sarno found himself flooded with paperwork in the early 1970s, the result of the rapidly increasing number of manufacturers' coupons being redeemed at his store by customers seeking to stretch their food budgets in the face of rising inflation. Desperate, Sarno contacted the established clearinghouses that processed coupons for big supermarket chains like Kroger and Grand Union, but they turned him away because his volume was too small. Realizing from his "insider's perspective" that other independent grocers were experiencing the same problem, Sarno founded Seven Oaks International in 1971, a coupon clearinghouse specializing in small-volume accounts. Over the next 15 years, Seven Oaks grew into a major diversified clearinghouse, handling both independents and chains, and second in volume only to longtime industry leader A. C. Nielsen.

Of course, we do not intend to imply that the advantages we have described here as age assets are possessed exclusively by those over 40. The younger entrepreneur can have a sense of confidence that is just as unshakable or a reputation just as respected as his or her older counterpart's. However, because advantages like confidence and a strong professional reputation are the products of time and experience, they tend to be present to a greater degree in the older entrepreneur.

Experience is, after all, the best teacher, and those over 40 have spent more time under its tutelage. Entrepreneurs who are able to apply their experience to a mid-life business venture will often find that the best is indeed yet to come.

1. *Joseph Tushinsky (right) and his younger brother, Fred, introduce the new Sony 760 tape recorder at a trade show. A former trumpeter with Toscanini's NBC Orchestra, Tushinsky brought the first Sony recorder to the U.S. in 1957. He remained the sole North American importer of the machine for the next 22 years. (Photo by Joseph Wayne)*

I

*Drawing
an Ace*

Frank D. Hickingbotham *(1936–   )*

TCBY ENTERPRISES, INC.

"The time was right for a national frozen yogurt chain."

Frank Hickingbotham did not have an original idea in October 1981, when he opened a frozen yogurt store in his hometown of Little Rock, Arkansas. Yogurt stands had been popping up in American cities since the mid-1970s in response to the growing demand for a healthy alternative to ice cream.

The 45-year-old entrepreneur did not even have an original product. His new store served the same yogurt that he and his wife had always enjoyed at the Neiman-Marcus lunch counter on their frequent business trips to Dallas.

But like Ray Kroc, who invented neither the hamburger nor the fast food restaurant, Hickingbotham's genius lay not in originating a new food concept, but in developing the marketing and management plans needed to turn a good idea into an immensely profitable business. His TCBY Enterprises, Inc. became the first company to apply McDonald's-like franchising and merchandising techniques to the frozen yogurt industry.

In so doing, the quiet, unassuming southerner created one of the most sensational success stories in the history of food franchising. After ringing up systemwide retail sales of $1.8 million in 1982, its first full year in business, TCBY's store sales have jumped to $5.2 million in 1983, $11.5 million in 1984, $34.1 million in 1985, $70 million in 1986, and a projected $130 million in 1987. Hickingbotham's 45 percent share of his public company was worth over $160 million in late 1986.[1]

Unlike McDonald's founder, Kroc, who had been through an up-and-down career as a musician and salesman before entering the hamburger business, Hickingbotham was already affluent when he started TCBY, having enjoyed considerable success as an insurance agent, restaurateur, and food manufacturer. In fact, he was ready to take an early retirement at 44, after selling his Dallas-based cake mix company, when he decided "on a lark" to open a frozen yogurt store.

"I kid people and tell them that I wanted something to do on my way to the golf course every day," remarked Hickingbotham. "Actually, I wanted to start a new business here in Little Rock after I sold my cake mix company, and the idea of a store that sold the same frozen yogurt as Neiman-Marcus seemed very appealing.

"My wife and I had been enjoying the yogurt for about a year whenever we were in Dallas. I was amazed at how good it tasted; it was very superior to any frozen yogurt that I had ever run across."

After making arrangements with Neiman-Marcus' yogurt supplier, Hickingbotham invested $40,000 to start his own store, This Can't Be Yogurt. He was later forced to change his stores' name to The Country's Best Yogurt, after a competitor, I Can't Believe It's Yogurt, Inc., took him to court. The settlement cost Hickingbotham $775,000, the only significant setback his frozen yogurt company has experienced.

Hickingbotham's first store, managed by his son Herren, was such a success that he quickly opened a second location in North Little Rock and hired his brother-in-law, Walt Winters, as manager. A few months later, he added a third store in nearby Conway, Arkansas, managed by his youngest son, Todd.

By the spring of 1982, Hickingbotham faced a major decision: he could continue to run TCBY as a successful but small local chain, or he could capitalize on the opportunity to get in on the ground floor of what promised to be a booming national industry.

"The time was right for a national frozen yogurt chain, and if we didn't do it someone else would," he recalled. "I talked the matter over with my family, and they agreed that they wanted to continue with it and work at building the company."

A bright, analytical man, who had prospered as an insurance agent planning estates for wealthy farmers, Hickingbotham followed a strategy of "getting biggest fastest" to establish TCBY as the dominant player in the frozen yogurt market. This strategy had enabled other fast food entrepreneurs like Ray Kroc and Tom Monaghan of Domino's Pizza to build early, and virtually insurmountable, leads in their markets. It worked equally well for the TCBY founder. In March 1985, TCBY had 118 stores scattered throughout the country,[2] while its next-largest competitor, Zack's Famous Frozen Yogurt of New Orleans, had 40 locations. By the end of 1986, the number of TCBY stores had increased to 500, located in every state except North Dakota and Vermont.

This geometric expansion was achieved through franchising, a business practice that Hickingbotham had become very familiar with during the early 1970s, when he operated and sold fried chicken franchises in Arkansas. In 1987, all but six percent of TCBY's stores were owned by franchisees, who pay the company a four percent royalty on sales and a three percent advertising fund contribution. The average franchisee invests $100,000 to open a TCBY store. Franchisees also buy yogurt from TCBY, which acquired the Neiman-Marcus supplier's factory.

Hickingbotham lists "quality franchisees" as one of the three key factors behind the growth of his company. (The others are a "unique product" and "good central office management.") He takes obvious pride in the fact that TCBY has "never advertised for franchisees in magazines, at trade shows, or anyplace else." All new franchisees contact the company as a result of referrals or after patronizing one of its stores. TCBY has also been successful at selling additional locations to existing franchisees. In 1986, approximately 75 percent of all new locations were opened by people who already owned a TCBY store.

The most famous TCBY franchisee is Mickey Rooney, who owns a store in the Hollywood area. In 1986, Hickingbotham signed the veteran actor as a television ad spokesman for the company. The TV commercials, which will be built around the marketing theme "All of the pleasure, none of the guilt," are part of a campaign to create greater name recognition for the company.

2. Tall, reserved, and methodical, TCBY founder Frank Hickingbotham provides a sharp contrast to the frozen yogurt company's most famous franchisee, Mickey Rooney.

In 1986, Hickingbotham also formed TCBY International, Inc. to franchise yogurt stores in other countries. The Arkansas centimillionaire expects to open 400 new locations in the U.S. and overseas in 1987.

Although much of TCBY's growth can indeed be attributed to the efforts of its franchisees and the quality of its product, these provide only a partial explanation for the company's success. Of no less significance are the marketing skills of Frank Hickingbotham. By expanding quickly, the TCBY founder was able to corner important markets like Houston, Atlanta, and Los Angeles before potential competitors could mount a serious challenge. TCBY's size also allowed the company to be a more aggressive advertiser than its smaller competitors.

Hickingbotham further distinguished his company from the competition in 1984, when he took TCBY public, listing it on the National Market System exchange. The decision to become a public company accomplished two very important goals: 1) it allowed TCBY to raise the capital required to buy the Neiman-Marcus yogurt supplier and thereby control the quality and distribution of its product; and 2) it allowed the company to attract and retain talented central office executives by offering attractive stock options.

Frank Hickingbotham's most original contribution to the success of his company, however, did not involve franchising, public financing, or yogurt production, but his vision of how a frozen yogurt store should be marketed to the American public. Just as Ray Kroc changed the public's perception of the hamburger restaurant from a "greasy spoon" to a clean, wholesome place for suburban families, Hickingbotham built TCBY by creating a new image for yogurt stands.

Back in the 1970s, frozen yogurt stores typically had a "counterculture" look, with secondhand fixtures and tables, dim lighting, and unframed posters on the walls. Often located near a college campus or in an artist's loft district, most stores complemented their frozen yogurt with other health food staples like carrot juice, soy burgers, and carob cookies.

A frozen yogurt chain that hoped to capitalize on the public's growing health-consciousness would have to gear itself more toward mainstream American tastes. Frank Hickingbotham recognized this, and from the very beginning his plan was to model TCBY after ice cream store chains in terms of decor, site selection, and menu. The one major difference, of course, was that TCBY would serve yogurt, not ice cream.

All TCBY stores are decorated in the same green-and-beige scheme, colors chosen, according to Hickingbotham, because "they symbolize naturalness and health." This message is reinforced by natural wood grain tables, fresh-flower centerpieces, wicker chairs, and hanging plants. TCBY stores are located primarily in strip shopping centers, where they are readily accessible to suburban customers.

Unlike its early yogurt stand predecessors, TCBY sells only frozen yogurt products. The company's Dallas plant produces frozen yogurt in twenty-one flavors, from the traditional French vanilla, chocolate, and strawberry to the exotic kiwi, watermelon, and blueberry cheesecake. Between four and six different flavors are served at a store at any one time. Frozen yogurt is delivered to TCBY stores by Martin-Brower, a large and efficient restaurant chain distributor that services only thirteen other companies—including McDonald's.

TCBY stores serve frozen yogurt in cups and waffle cones, as well as in shakes, sundaes, and banana splits. The stores also sell frozen yogurt pies, yogurt-cookie sandwiches, yogurt-and-waffles, and yogurt-crepe specialties. "We offer all of the fun and variety of the old-fashioned ice cream store, but we make all the dishes with frozen yogurt," explained Hickingbotham.

TCBY franchisees do a minimal amount of food preparation. Frozen yogurt arrives at a store from the Dallas factory in final form. The franchisee then thaws the product and pours it into mixing machines for refreezing before it is served. The only foods actually made in-store are daily batches of fresh waffles and waffle cones.

By limiting the scope of TCBY's menu and keeping in-store food preparation to a minimum, Hickingbotham has increased the operating efficiency of his frozen yogurt stores. He has also made it a great deal easier for franchisees to maintain a clean store environment. This was a lesson he learned after years in the restaurant business. "When you do a lot of food preparation and frying, it becomes much more difficult to keep your restaurant clean. This is one reason why I wanted to keep things simple at the yogurt stores."

Although he was considering an early retirement before he started TCBY, Frank Hickingbotham now dismisses any notion of stepping down as chairman and president of the frozen yogurt company. "I don't think I could ever retire—I have no interest in the retirement-type of life. Every morning I'm at the office at seven-thirty, and I leave at around six. I really enjoy my work."

Hickingbotham is often amused by those who congratulate him on his "overnight success." "People will come up to me and tell me how lucky I was to have succeeded so quickly. I always tell them that I've been building this company for twenty years. The experiences I've had, good and bad, laid the groundwork for my success."

Born in the small southeastern Arkansas town of McGehee, Hickingbotham's first significant career experience occurred when he returned home, four years after his graduation from college, to become the principal of the local junior high school. "My first day on the job was pretty scary," he recalled. "A lot of the teachers I was supervising had taught me when I was in school. One of the first things I did was hold a meeting and say to them, 'Now we're going to see what kind of job you did teaching me.' From that moment on, they were on my side!"

After four years as principal, Hickingbotham's annual salary was only $4200, so he resigned to seek a more lucrative career as an insurance agent. He left the insurance business in 1969 to become head of Quality Enterprises, a restaurant and food manufacturing firm that he and a group of associates had started a few years earlier. During the 1970s, Hickingbotham became involved in a number of restaurant franchising and food processing businesses. Then in 1979 he purchased the Old Tyme Foods Company, the Dallas cake mix manufacturer.

"Living in Little Rock, I had to travel to Dallas to oversee the cake mix business," said Hickingbotham. "On one trip, my wife visited Neiman-Marcus, where she tasted the frozen yogurt. She kept telling me how good it was, so finally I went to the store with her to try it for myself ... "

The rest, as they say, is history.

Bill LeVine *(1920–)*

POSTAL INSTANT PRESS

"I saw a good opportunity and I jumped in."

Instant printing pioneer Bill LeVine regards opportunity like a train. If you stand on the station platform long enough, sooner or later you will see the small, silent speck of a locomotive appear on the horizon. The speck will grow bigger and louder, until, by the time it reaches the station, it becomes impossible to ignore. Then you face a choice: jump on board and let the train carry you away, or remain at the station and watch it retreat into the distance.

LeVine saw his opportunity roll in back in 1964, when he chanced upon a new offset printing technology. Hopping on board with both feet, he turned this discovery into Postal Instant Press, an 1100-unit chain of instant print shops that has emerged as the dominant player in a $3.9 billion industry.

Most people in LeVine's position at the time would have been unwilling to gamble on a new opportunity. The 44-year-old owner of a moderately successful ($1.5 million volume) commercial printing plant in Los Angeles, he enjoyed all the trappings of the Southern California Good Life: a big house, new cars, frequent travel.

This was a far cry from the rather dreary circumstances of LeVine's Los Angeles childhood. One of eight children of Russian-Jewish parents, he began working after school at 11 years of age, following the death of his father, to help provide his family with the barest necessities. He had worked hard ever since, and had finally achieved a measure of comfort and security. The temptation to play it safe must have been great.

"I didn't need the money; I had a good little business, and I could have sat back and let it run itself," he recalled. "But I'm an entrepreneur at heart. I saw a good opportunity and I jumped in."

LeVine described how he came upon the entrepreneurial opportunity that changed his life. "I was returning home from a trip to Israel, and I stopped in New York to visit an old friend who had a dress design business in the garment district. He showed me a new Itek commercial camera that he was using to make pictures of his designs. He would print these pictures on a small offset press and distribute them to buyers in New York."

Although his friend's camera process yielded results that were only fair in quality by commercial printing standards, it did offer two important advantages over conventional offset printing: speed and economy. Traditional offset printing involved a costly and elaborate eight-step process that transferred images from film to "flats" to metal plates. The new two-step camera process, on the other hand, produced a paper plate that was ready for printing in only 55 seconds.

The new method opened the door to an entirely new group of printing customers, a group that had never been reached by commercial printing plants. "Commercial printers like me catered to large-order accounts: a supermarket that wanted thousands of circulars or a big chain that wanted to blanket the city with handbills," said LeVine. "A sales rep who wanted a few hundred business cards or a storeowner who wanted to print up some announcements couldn't use us, because the offset process was too expensive for his small order. Basically, he was stuck with a mimeograph or some other inadequate method of printing his material. Then, this new technology came along and made it economically practical to print small orders while still maintaining a good level of quality."

As Bill LeVine would later discover, reaching the small-order customer would not only require a new offset printing technology, but an entirely new merchandising approach on the part of the printing industry. The dreary, low-rent warehouse structures that most printers occupied were adequate for serving large commercial accounts, but they put off the small-order customer, who, as a conventional consumer, was accustomed to shopping at more convenient and attractive retail locations. The printer who hoped to capture the instant printing market would have to take his service to the customer by opening bright, well-staffed stores in high-traffic shopping areas. In short, he would have to become as much retailer as printer. It was precisely this realization that would eventually lead Bill LeVine to launch a new career in a very new and different kind of industry.

But back when he was visiting his friend's dress design studio, LeVine was too enthralled with the technological advantages of the new camera-offset process to worry much about its marketing implications. Upon returning home to California, he purchased a $4500 Itek camera and began experimenting with ways to improve its performance through the use of different inks and chemicals. A year later, he perfected a process that worked far better than his friend's small press had in New York.

LeVine was not the only commercial printer experimenting with the new Itek camera in the mid-1960s. Other printers in other parts of the country were doing similar work and coming up with equally good results. But the thin, deep-voiced Californian was the first to recognize instant printing as a separate and distinct business from commercial printing, and, of even greater importance, he was the first to act on this new opportunity on a large scale.

In January 1967, after about a year of test marketing the new instant printing service at his west Los Angeles commercial plant, LeVine and his wife Bonny opened the first Postal Instant Press store in Westwood. Within six months, the couple had two additional stores: one on Sunset Strip, the other at the intersection of Wilshire and Vermont, a site chosen because of its proximity to many insurance offices and other small businesses. All of the stores sported prominent Postal Instant Press signs.

"Choosing the name Postal Instant Press was easy," recalled LeVine. "Our original printing business was called Postal Press, because it specialized in printing postcards, so all we did was add the word 'instant.' Then Bonny came up with the idea of calling ourselves 'PIP,' because it looks good on signs and is kind of catchy."

The three original PIP stores were just beginning to establish themselves in the Los Angeles market in October 1967 when a friend suggested that LeVine rent a booth at a local franchise show. LeVine was reluctant at first, arguing that instant printing was "not a franchisable concept," but the friend persisted and LeVine finally agreed to take a booth. It was a decision that he would never have cause to regret.

"The interest in our booth was unbelievable," said LeVine. "We signed up three franchise owners [he doesn't use the word "franchisee"] at the show, and they all opened stores in 1968. By the end of 1969, we had sixty-five franchised PIP stores."

Like Frank Hickingbotham, who has come to rule the frozen yogurt industry by opening a large number of TCBY outlets in a short time before serious competition could enter the market, LeVine came to dominate the instant printing business by quickly blanketing the nation with PIP stores. The number of PIP stores increased rapidly: 273 in 1975, 571 in 1980, and 1006 in 1985.

Virtually all of this expansion was accomplished with franchised locations. At one time, PIP owned forty outlets, but today only two of its 1100 stores in the U.S., Canada, Europe, and Japan are company-owned. "You can't serve two masters," explained LeVine. "Our strength is in franchising, and this is where we decided to concentrate our efforts. Much of the success that we've enjoyed has been due to our ability to attract quality franchise owners."

Although PIP advertises in the business opportunities section of the *Wall Street Journal* and other publications, about 70 percent of all new franchisees come as a result of referrals from existing store owners. After a prospective franchisee's application has been accepted by the company, he undergoes an intensive training program in Los Angeles. When the novice franchisee shows up at his own PIP store for the first time, he will find a smiling PIP franchise support representative waiting for him, ready to warm up the printing press, brew some coffee, and lend some encouragement. The support representative remains at the new store for one week, but should the franchisee encounter any difficulty, help is as close as the nearest telephone.

"Franchising is a hand-holding business," said Bill LeVine. "At times, Bonny and I have been like parents to the franchise owners, helping them with problems, giving them advice and encouragement. We knew every franchise owner and his or her spouse by name up until the time we passed 500 stores."

Despite the size of their organization, the LeVines still manage to maintain a sense of camaraderie among PIP franchisees. They publish a bimonthly magazine, *PIPline,* that contains upbeat news about the company and its franchisees, and a monthly listing of operating tips submitted by franchisees called "PIPers Exchange." They also hold regional meetings and workshops, as well as a biennial "International Conclave." A three-day event, the conclave features seminars, product exhibits, awards ceremonies ("Friendliest PIPer"), and a talent show put on by franchisees.

The LeVines' efforts at educating and motivating franchisees have helped PIP maintain a very low rate of store failures. Fewer than two percent of the company's locations have closed since it began franchising. In recognition of its achievements as a franchisor, PIP was honored as the first recipient of the International Franchise Association's annual Franchisee Relations Award in 1985.

PIP's interest in its franchisees stems from more than pure altruism. As Bill LeVine explains: "Taking care of our franchise owners isn't just being nice, it's being smart. The franchise owners are our customers, and their success is our success. We don't make money selling products to our franchise owners. We make some money selling franchises and on the interest from our franchise-financing, but our big income comes from royalties on our franchise owners' sales. So we have a vested interest in seeing them do well."

How did Bill LeVine, a man with no previous experience in franchising, become, after the age of 47, one of America's most successful and respected franchisors? He believes that the answer has a lot to do with his background as a commercial printer. Early in his career, he learned that there was no real difference in quality between the supermarket circulars printed at one plant or another. The difference lay in the level of service that each plant provided: How fast did it get the job done? Did it stand behind its work? Did it deliver finished work as promised?

Like a commercial printer, a franchisor is also selling reliability and service. Will he provide the promised advertising support? How complete is his training program? Will he be there if the franchisee runs into problems? Bill LeVine simply transferred the service orientation he had developed as a commercial printer to his new role as a franchisor of instant printing shops.

LeVine has been involved in printing for most of his 66 years. "I took print shop in junior high school, and after that I saved money from my paper route to buy a small hand-fed press. This was not just a hobby; I needed to make money to help my family get by. My big account at that time was the West Jefferson Cleaners. I printed and distributed ten thousand handbills for them every week, working on weekends and after school. I didn't have time for sports or anything like that; all my free time after school was devoted to work."

Following graduation from high school in 1939, LeVine worked briefly for a shoe repair business before returning to printing as an outside salesman for the Coast Stationery Company. Then came a 72-day stint in the Navy in 1942—he was discharged because of a bad back—before he started his own commercial printing plant on $3000 borrowed from a brother.

"I would call on accounts to sell orders by day, and then I would print them in the evening," he recalled. "I made a living, and that was about it. My wife worked at Lockheed, and we needed the paycheck she brought home. Then the business began to grow, and by the time PIP was started, the commercial plant was doing very well. Of course, it was not big at all next to the success we've enjoyed at PIP."

Deeply tanned, with a full head of snow white hair and a smile as big and bright as a California sunrise, Bill LeVine could pass for a Hollywood producer. The only physical evidence of his early struggles is a mashed index finger, the result of an encounter with an unfriendly hand-fed press.

In 1985, LeVine turned over the presidency of PIP, an American Stock Exchange company, to Thomas C. Marotto, a former Xerox executive. The transition of power continued in 1986, when Marotto became CEO, with LeVine remaining as board chairman.

"When a company gets to a certain size, the entrepreneur can't run things the way he did at one time," LeVine explained. "At that point it makes sense to bring in a professional manager."

Although he has relinquished many of his responsibilities, LeVine is still very involved in PIP and the company's plans for

21

the future. He sees PIP stores emerging as communications centers for small businesspeople by providing facsimile transmission, overnight mail, word processing, and similar services. "The
small businessperson isn't going to pull in all [this] equipment,"
he told *The Franchise Advisor* magazine. "It's going to take a service such as PIP to offer [this] to the small businessperson."[1]

Facsimile transmission? Word processing? At 66, entrepreneur Bill LeVine is still looking for new opportunities, and still
ready to hop on board when they stop at his station.

David Mullany *(1908–)*

WIFFLE BALL, INC.

"I wanted to control my own company."

As a pitcher on the University of Connecticut's varsity base-ball team in the late 1920s, David Mullany sometimes dreamed of playing in the big leagues, perhaps for the Yankees or Red Sox, his two favorite teams.

The strong left-hander never made it to the majors, playing only a few seasons of semi-pro ball with the Bridgeport Yankees, but he did leave his mark on a modified version of the national pastime by inventing the Wiffle Ball.

In the thirty-odd years since Mullany carved the first Wiffle Ball in the kitchen of his Fairfield, Connecticut, home, the per-forated white plastic sphere—which was described by *Esquire* magazine,[1] as "a national treasure"—has become almost as much a part of American life as the conventional baseball that inspired it.

The unimposing Wiffle Ball factory in Shelton, Connecticut, turns out millions of balls a year under the watchful eyes of Mul-lany and his son, David, Jr. This entire output is snatched up by players eager to test their Wiffle skills in city schoolyards, sub-urban backyards, college campuses, office parking lots, beaches, and just about anyplace else that affords the small amount of space required for an impromptu game.

The humble Wiffle Ball has even turned up at the White House. According to the authors of *The Final Days,* some of Rich-

3. Former college pitcher David
Mullany created the Wiffle Ball
in 1953 for his son's backyard
games.

ard Nixon's aides escaped the pressures of the Watergate crisis
by playing Wiffle home run derby on the presidential tennis
court.

Americans value the Wiffle Ball for the things it does: curve
and dip more precipitously than a mountain road, without requiring arm contortions on the part of the pitcher; and for the
things it does not do: go very far, injure players, or break windows.

In fact, it was these considerations that prompted Mullany to
create the Wiffle Ball in the summer of 1953. "My father made
the first Wiffle Ball so my buddies and I could play backyard
games without causing undue damage to ourselves or our sur-
roundings," said David Mullany, Jr.

The younger Mullany, who was 12 at the time, had started the
summer playing the traditional hardball variety of baseball.

"We'd go to the local ball field early every day, but sooner or
later the big kids would show up and throw us out," he recounted. "Then we started playing in each others' yards, but this
had to stop when we broke some garage windows."

Prohibited from using hardballs, David and his friends im-
provised games with tennis balls, Spaldenes, and plastic golf balls.
The golf balls quickly emerged as the most popular hardball sub-

stitute because a pitcher could, by violently snapping his wrist, make them dip and curve in tantalizingly eccentric patterns.

After an hour or two of throwing this way, David's arm would "feel like jelly." This, of course, came as no surprise to his father. As a former pitcher, the senior Mullany was well aware of the damage that whipping curve ball deliveries could inflict on young tendons.

Not wishing to see the boy injure his arm, Mullany resolved to create a plastic ball that would dip and bend without much coaxing from the pitcher. He went to a local factory and obtained a supply of hollow plastic spheres that had been used as Christmas packages for Coty perfume. When he returned home, he set the spheres out on the kitchen table and cut different configurations of holes into each one with a razor knife.

"He hoped that the holes would put more movement into the ball's path," explained David Mullany, Jr. "When we tried out the different balls the next day, most of them didn't do anything but float harmlessly across the plate."

There was one exception, though: a ball with eight oblong holes cut into one of its hemispheres that curved wickedly without any wrist snapping. David and his friends called the ball a "wiffle ball," after the taunt they hurled at every batter who struck out before its perplexing curve, "I whiffed you."

The Mullanys do not have an aerodynamic explanation for the success of the Wiffle Ball's eight-oblong-hole design. "We don't know why this particular design works, and we've never had the slightest interest in having it analyzed," said David Mullany, Jr. "All we know is that it does work, and from day one, it's been the design we've used on all Wiffle Balls."

Creating a safe plaything for his son was not the only thing that David Mullany had in mind when he fashioned the first Wiffle Ball in 1953. As a partner in a foundering car polish business, he was looking for a new venture to fall back on in the event that his company failed.

When the polish business reached its inevitable demise in 1954, Mullany borrowed about $20,000 from some friends ("the banks wouldn't loan me money") and started Wiffle Ball. "These friends were not investors, you understand," said Mullany, his usually flat voice rising slightly. "They only loaned me money. I didn't want investors; I wanted to control my own company."

In keeping with its founder's independent spirit, Wiffle Ball, Inc., is still run like an overgrown New England cottage industry. Its "factory" is a modest brick building about the size of a four-car garage, located next to a motorcycle shop. Its most distinguishing feature is the sign in front: an eight-foot replica of a Wiffle Ball.

Inside, the company's office has a worn, neglected look, its walls paneled with a synthetic wood grain particle board and its four large desks covered with papers and product samples. The production area, though small, is a model of efficiency, with impressive plastic molding equipment coughing up a new Wiffle Ball every five seconds.

Although he has semi-retired to Florida and turned the day-to-day operations of the company over to his son, the 78-year-old Mullany still shows up at the Shelton plant about six months a year. "He enjoys coming here and is very much involved in running the business," said David Mullany, Jr., who came to work at the plant full time in 1962.

The Mullanys have received many attractive buyout offers over the years, but they have never been tempted to sell Wiffle Ball. "You hate to let go of something that you worked so hard to start," explained David Mullany.

Wiffle Ball is indeed the product of a herculean effort on the part of its founder. A factory of any kind was beyond the company's reach in the early days, so Mullany farmed out production of the balls to an outside plant. After he had made his sales calls for the day, he would pick up balls from the plant and go to a small "warehouse" to package orders for shipment.

"I didn't have the money for employees, so I did everything myself, even if it meant putting in 12- or 14-hour days. This was a pretty scary time, but I had a feeling about the ball—a good feeling. Right after I started, I put a display case of Wiffle Balls in a restaurant off the Merritt Parkway in New Haven on consignment. The restaurant owner put the case by his cash register, hoping that he could sell a few balls to kids who came there with their parents. Within a month, he was moving a gross of Wiffle Balls a week. This sort of proved to me that I was onto something big."

Unfortunately, the toy buyers at department stores and variety chains did not share Mullany's enthusiasm. For more than

4. Although sales were slow at first, the Wiffle Ball became one of the country's hottest toy products by the end of the decade. The ball's 8-ob-long-hole design makes it easy to curve without violent wrist contortions.

two years, he tried without success to get major retailers to carry the unusual lightweight ball.

Then he hired Saul Mondschein, a veteran New York toy sales representative. Working his industry connections, Mondschein got the Wiffle Ball into Woolworth's and other big retail chains, transforming the product into one of the hot fad items of the 1950s. The demand for Wiffle Balls had become so great by 1958 that Mullany was able to build the Shelton factory and take over production directly.

"Our sales rose very quickly in the fifties," said David Mullany, Jr. "At first we were strongest in the big cities in the East and Midwest, because this was where space for real baseball fields was scarcest, and where all of the pro teams were located at the time.

"Then, as the major leagues expanded into cities like Los Angeles, San Francisco, and Houston, Wiffle Ball became more popular in the West and South. Wherever you had a good pro team, you had a good Wiffle Ball market."

In the early 1960s, the Mullanys tried to capitalize on this baseball connection by running TV commercials starring Whitey Ford in selected cities. It was their first, and last, attempt at media advertising. Although sales rose in markets where the commercials were aired, the increase was not large enough to defray the costs of advertising.

"We felt that we had a good, quality product that sold itself to kids, so we didn't see the point of continuing with the TV commercials, which were very expensive anyway," said Mullany.

The only continuing form of advertising that the Mullanys have done is to put the likenesses of major league ballplayers on Wiffle Ball packages. Their first endorsees were Ted Williams, Whitey Ford, Jackie Jensen, and Eddie Mathews.

"I don't know if having ballplayers on the box has helped our sales any, but it's kind of a tradition, and it costs us very little," said David Mullany, Jr.

By limiting their advertising, eschewing a fancy office in a high-rent venue, and continuously improving the efficiency of their production line, the Mullanys have been able to defy the effects of inflation. A regulation-sized Wiffle Ball that retailed for 50 cents in 1955 could still be bought for under a dollar in 1986.

"We think that we offer one of the best toy values in America," declared David Mullany. "What else can a kid buy for under a dollar that will give him this much fun? This is why we've always been slow to change things; why tamper with a winner?"

The Mullanys have tried marketing Wiffle Footballs and Wiffle Basketballs, but both products were dropped for lack of sales. "People think of baseball when they think of Wiffle Ball," explained David, Jr. "The other sports just didn't fit our image."

Wiffle Ball's most successful attempt at diversification has been the Wiffle Bat. The company began selling bats after it opened its Shelton factory in 1958. Its original bats were nothing more than sawed-off broomsticks with black electrical tape wrapped around one end to form the handle. Mullany later purchased a lathe and began manufacturing "fungo-style" wooden bats.

The familiar yellowish plastic Wiffle Bat first appeared in the early 1960s, after escalating lumber prices forced the company out of the wooden bat business. The Mullanys farm out the production of Wiffle Bats to outside factories, just as they do their other nonball products, Wiffle Bases and the Wiffle Flying Saucer, an imitation Frisbee.

"We've always been more interested in making a limited

number of products well than in adding new items left and right just for the sake of diversifying," said Mullany. "If we were going to diversify in a big way, it would mean going to the banks for capital or bringing in outside investors, and we wouldn't want that."

David Mullany acquired his conservative philosophy during a childhood spent on his family farm in Hattfield, Massachusetts. After starring on his high school's baseball team, Mullany went off to Connecticut, where, in addition to becoming a varsity pitcher, he earned a degree in economics. Following graduation in June 1929, he took a job with General Electric in Bridgeport.

"Then the stock market crashed in October, and since I was among the last hired, I was one of the first to be fired. Not too long after this, I became a purchasing agent for McKesson-Robbins [a pharmaceutical company]. This job really helped to prepare me for Wiffle Ball. It taught me basic management principles and gave me experience dealing with outside suppliers."

Of course, the fact that Mullany was a collegiate and semi-pro pitcher also had a great deal to do with his founding of Wiffle Ball. A father who was not as familiar with baseball would have been less aware of the threat that a sharp curve ball delivery posed to his son's arm.

But, like baseball, where bloop singles sometimes win pennants, the "game" of business is not without an element of chance.

"I was fortunate in that I started Wiffle Ball at exactly the right time," observed Mullany. "It would be much more difficult to do what I did today, because the toy industry is so different. Back in the fifties, the toy industry was made up of a lot of mom 'n pop outfits; a guy with a good idea could come in and do well if he worked hard. But that's all changed: now the industry is all big corporations. There isn't room for the one-product company run by a small group of individuals."

Alfred J. Roach (1915–   )

TII INDUSTRIES, INC.

"There are still so many new ideas to be tried."

At 71, TII Industries founder Al Roach has everything that a "poor kid from Harlem" could possibly want: beautiful homes in New York and Puerto Rico, access to some of the most powerful people in Washington, and a personal fortune reputed to be worth over $20 million.

Most men in his position would have slowed down long ago to savor the rewards of success, but the plucky white-haired entrepreneur waves off the notion of retirement, recalling a story about Picasso.

"When Picasso was in his later years, someone asked him, 'Why do you keep painting; you've already achieved so much, why not take it easy?' Do you know what he said? 'I keep painting because there are still so many blank canvases to be filled.'

"Well, that's how I feel about business. There are still so many new ideas to be tried, so many challenges to meet. Business is a creative experience for me, and I don't ever want to retire."

It was Roach's ability to recognize the market potential of a British invention in the early 1960s that led him to create the "masterpiece" of his career—TII Industries, a $40 million American Stock Exchange company. The British device was an "overvoltage protector," a small gas tube that grounds sudden surges in power caused by lightning or malfunctioning electrical systems before they can damage telephone equipment. The only other overvoltage protectors available at the time, carbon filament models, were far less durable and effective than the British gas tubes.

Seated in his office at TII's plant in Toa Alta, Puerto Rico, Roach recalled in a thick New York accent how he discovered the product that made him rich.

"I've always been a voracious reader of scientific magazines, and I remember one day I came across an article about how the new transistor telephones were going to require faster and better overvoltage protectors. A short time later, I was in England on business for an investment house when I learned about this gas tube protector."

In 1964, Roach bought the rights to the product from its developer, Associated Electronics Industries, for $60,000 cash. The 49-year-old entrepreneur returned home, set up a workshop in his Long Island basement, and hired a moonlighting engineer, Charles Roberts, to modify the device for the U.S. market.

"Charlie Roberts wound up working with me at TII for the remainder of his career, but back then he thought I was wasting my time trying to market a telecommunications product in this country. He warned me, 'If this is any good, the phone company will move right in and come up with a similar product for themselves.'"

Roach's brother-in-law, a New York phone company employee, took an even dimmer view of the new venture. Said Roach, "He told me I was out of my mind."

Indeed, TII seemed to be taking on an impossible task by challenging AT&T's equipment-making subsidiary, Western Electric, in the pre-deregulation era. But Al Roach had grown accustomed to waging uphill fights against bigger foes early in life.

"In Harlem, you had a choice—you could either run from trouble, talk your way out of it, or fight your way out of it. My legs were too short to run, so I did a lot of talking and fighting."

After dropping out of high school at the end of his first year, Roach bounced around from one manual laborer's job to another before enlisting in the Army at 17, lying to the recruiting officer about his age. He continued to sharpen his pugilistic skills in the service as a member of the Army boxing team, winning the welterweight championship title of the Pacific. From boxing, Roach learned the importance of persistence, a lesson that would later prove invaluable in business.

"There's a poem by Edgar Guest that I used to like when I was a boxer that exhorts you to 'keep going, keep going because the other fellow's getting tired too.' This is exactly how I fought; I was knocked down on occasion but never knocked out. I always got up, because I knew that if I kept going, the other guy would get tired and I would eventually win."

Al Roach needed every ounce of this persistence in the early days of TII. For almost two years, it seemed as if the skeptics had been right; AT&T refused even to consider his gas tube protector.

Then Roach decided to market his protector to the small, independent phone companies that serviced rural areas. But even with the independents, he encountered a wall of resistance to the new product. Carbon filament protectors had been used for years; they worked reasonably well, and, most importantly, they cost one-fifth as much as Roach's $10 devices.

"It might seem pretty crazy to ask someone who's been spending a couple of dollars a protector to all of a sudden pay $10 for one, but I had some convincing arguments," said Roach. "Not only were my protectors far superior in their performance, they didn't need to be replaced nearly as often as carbon filaments. A phone company would have to pay a repairman $25 or $30, or more, to go out and replace a $2 filament. Wouldn't it make more sense to spend $10 on a protector that didn't need frequent replacement? This became even more obvious as the cost of labor kept rising."

Finally, in the late 1960s, Roach convinced General Telephone and Electronics (GTE) to test his protectors in a high-lightning area on the Gulf Coast. The independent phone company reported a 90 to 97 percent reduction in surge-related repair and maintenance costs in markets where TII's gas tube protectors were installed.

When the results of the GTE test were made public, TII found itself flooded with orders from independent phone companies. Even AT&T-affiliated companies ordered protectors for high-priority lines such as those to police and fire stations, although some of this business was later lost when Western Electric introduced its own gas tube protector.

In 1975, Roach moved his growing company's manufacturing operation to a former Curtis Mathes TV plant in Toa Alta, Puerto Rico, keeping his executive offices on Long Island. He began marketing gas tube protectors internationally two years later, after signing a licensing agreement with Sweden's LM Ericsson.

TII's fortunes received their biggest boost in 1984, when AT&T's Bell System was broken up by deregulation. With their connection to Western Electric severed, local phone companies were able to shop more freely for equipment, allowing independent suppliers like TII to compete with the Bell System's former manufacturing subsidiary on an equal footing. This had the expected healthy effect on TII's balance sheet: revenues jumped from $23.4 million in 1983 to $40 million in 1986.

As his original gas tube protector business grew, Al Roach diversified into other ventures. In 1984, he co-founded, with Notre Dame University, American Biogenetic Sciences, Inc., to develop a therapeutic agent that uses the body's own enzymes to dissolve blood clots. Another Roach company is TeleProbe, Inc., the producer of a very successful product that automatically locates the source of malfunctions in large telephone systems.

"I have always been interested in new ideas," said Roach. "It's not my style to sit back and play it safe. Every morning I jump out of bed eager to start my day, because there are so many new things waiting to be done."

Of course, not all of Al Roach's new ideas have worked out. In the early 1970s, he poured $3 million into a project to develop a water purification system that used ozone gas instead of conventional chlorine, only to discover that ozone was too costly to gain commercial acceptance.

Still, the essence of entrepreneurship is risk, and Al Roach shrugs off business reversals with the calm certitude of a boxer who knows that he will be back to fight another day. "Sure, failure hurts—but it shouldn't stop you from trying. If I went broke tomorrow, I'd get right back up and try again. You learn from all of your experiences—good and bad. This is why I think it's easier to start a business when you're older; you've had all that experience, and that's made you a lot smarter."

Indeed, no business school could have provided an education as rich in diversity as the one Roach received from his own peripatetic experience. After leaving the Army, he moved from job to job, working as a Kentucky field hand, a merchant marine, an insurance salesman, a loan officer, and the president of a small brewery in upstate New York.

In the early 1960s, Roach was making well over $50,000 a year as a stockbroker when he gambled his future on the new gas tube protector. Was he scared? "You bet I was. I had some early morning risings with a sinking feeling in my stomach, wondering how I was ever going to get the money to meet my payroll."

Even though Roach's ultimate success was greatly enhanced by the break-up of the phone company, the feisty New Yorker was adamantly opposed to the AT&T divestiture.

"I had my run-ins with AT&T in the past; at one time I came very close to suing them myself. But when I was called on to testify at the divestiture hearing in Washington, I made it very clear that I was against the Balkanization of one of the best-run, most successful companies in the world. AT&T provided this country with the world's best phone system, a system that took a hundred years to build, but the government dismembered it for no apparent reason.

"The AT&T breakup is just another example of how the government is harassing business. The absolute worst people to put in charge of regulating business are government bureaucrats. What experience do they have in meeting a payroll? They take a very provincial view of the world: 'This is the way we think things should be, so all you American companies have to follow these regulations.' What they don't seem to realize is that we live in a world economy. Japan, Malaysia, and other countries don't have all of these regulations. So how is American industry supposed to compete? It is absolutely unbelievable how our government has failed to recognize the realities of the international marketplace."

Waking America up to what he perceives as the "realities" of the world economy has become a personal crusade for the TII founder. The U.S., according to Roach, is in real danger of becoming "a colonial dependency of Japan," a nation he accuses of using "subpaid labor to copy our computers, scientific instruments, machinery, motors, planes, automobiles . . . you name it."

In 1982, Roach spent $56,000 to buy full-page ads in the Sunday, January 24, *New York Times* and the Monday, January 25, *Washington Post* in order to send "An Urgent Message to the President and the Congress of the United States of America." In his message, Roach warned that the U.S. was losing an "undeclared war with Japan." He argued that before the tide could be turned, drastic improvements would have to be made in the government's method of regulating business, and in an American educational system that produced "ten thousand lawyers for every thousand engineers," compared to a Japanese system that turned out "a hundred lawyers for every thousand engineers."

The newspaper message drew responses from a variety of quarters. From the White House came word that President Reagan was "grateful for the many areas of common ground discussed in the text." From Congress came an invitation for Roach to testify before the House Ways and Means Subcommittee on

5. TII founder Alfred Roach is all smiles as he meets Vice-President George Bush during one of Roach's many visits to Washington to speak on behalf of the Caribbean Basin Initiative.

Trade. And from the Japanese government came a visit from ambassador Morizuki Motono, who flew to Puerto Rico for a three-hour meeting with the outspoken American.

For his part, Roach insists that he is not anti-Japanese. "I have nothing against Japan or the Japanese. In fact, I admire their tenacity; they'll go out and learn English. How many Americans do you know who will learn Japanese? They've done an excellent job in creating a good business environment. If there is a heaven for businessmen, the place they would go after they died would be Japan."

In 1984, Roach was back in Washington, appointed to a presidential task force established to evaluate the effects of the administration's Caribbean Basin Initiative. The septuagenarian executive, who has a plant in Haiti in addition to his Puerto Rico facility, endorsed the program wholeheartedly.

"Most of the world goes to bed hungry, and we can help change this by bringing jobs and industry to emerging countries. There will be tremendous challenges and opportunities in these countries in the future, and I wish that I could live another fifty years to be a part of it all."

Since becoming politically active, has Al Roach thought of running for office himself? "I've considered politics," he confessed, "but I decided against it. I enjoy business too much to ever give it up."

Joseph S. Tushinsky (1910–   )

SUPERSCOPE, INC.

"I knew that the Sony tape recorder couldn't miss in this country."

Joe Tushinsky, a gregarious 47-year-old Californian, went to Tokyo in 1957 to sell Japanese movie studios the "Superscope" wide screen process that he and his brother Irving had developed three years earlier. A devotee of classical music and operettas, Tushinsky looked forward to making a short side trip during his Japanese visit to the showroom of a little-known electronics firm called Tokyo Tsushin Kogyo (Tokyo Telecommunications). He had been told about a new, advanced condenser microphone made by the company and was eager to buy one for the hifi tape recorder he used back home in Los Angeles to record radio concerts.

Arriving at the "showroom" one day, the American businessman was dismayed by what he saw. "From the outside, the building didn't look like much, at least not by American standards. It was little more than a hut, certainly not the kind of place where you expected to find a technologically sophisticated electronics firm—even in 1957.

"Inside the showroom though, that was another story. After I bought my microphone, the people there showed me one of their new reel-to-reel stereophonic tape recorders. I was completely amazed! Back in America, we were still in the age of hifi. This was the first home stereophonic tape recorder that I had

37

ever heard, and the difference between it and my American machine was indescribable."

Tushinsky persuaded Akio Morita, one of the co-founders of the Japanese firm, to sell him six of the seven tape recorders on display in the showroom. "I wanted to buy all seven, but Mr. Morita insisted on keeping at least one, so he'd have something to show other customers."

Returning to Los Angeles, Tushinsky demonstrated the stereophonic recorder to enthusiastic crowds at local hifi-electronics stores. A month late, he was back in Tokyo, where he reached an agreement with Morita to become the exclusive North American and South American distributor of the Japanese company's tape recorder.

"At the time, the company was doing a $2000-a-month export business worldwide, and Mr. Morita was happy to grant me the Western Hemisphere rights at no charge," Tushinsky told the authors of this book. "I remember he was all excited because my name, 'Tu-shin-sky,' means 'to love electronics' in Japanese. He thought that this was a good omen."

The gods, indeed, must have been smiling on the Joseph Tushinsky–Tokyo Tsushin marriage. In the years that followed their 1957 agreement, the fortunes of both parties increased dramatically: the American became a millionaire many times over distributing the Japanese tape recorder, and Tokyo Tsushin grew into a major multinational electronics corporation under its new name—Sony.

It was no accident that Joe Tushinsky was able to recognize the potential of the innovative Japanese tape recorder he chanced upon in 1957. His understanding and appreciation of sound reproduction was highly developed as a result of his extensive musical background. Born in New York City, he studied music under his father, a noted viola player who performed with Arturo Toscanini's NBC Orchestra.

Joe Tushinsky exhibited an early talent for the trumpet, and at 18 he was earning $175 a week as assistant first trumpet with the St. Louis Fox Theatre Orchestra. This was followed by other, more prestigious, positions with orchestras in the East, until, in 1940, Tushinsky reached the pinnacle of his career as a trumpeter when he, too, became a member of Toscanini's orchestra. (His recollection of the Italian maestro: "A very good man who was obviously in a class by himself as a conductor—but he had one hell of a temper.")

Tushinsky left the NBC Orchestra in 1941 to form his own operetta troupe, The Papermill Playhouse Light Opera Company in Millburn, New Jersey. The company lasted only two seasons, but for Tushinsky it represented an important milestone. Now, for the first time, he wasn't simply a performer, but the producer and chief administrator of a musical performance company. This pointed his career in a new, more business-oriented direction— a direction that would eventually lead him to Sony.

As a result of his experience producing operettas, Tushinsky got involved in motion picture production. In 1943, he acquired the rights to the life story of songwriter Chauncey Olcott (*My Wild Irish Rose*), and made it into a Warner Brothers film starring Dennis Morgan. He later became an associate producer for Charles R. Rogers Productions in Hollywood and also wrote screenplays—most notably *Roxy's Life Story*.

In 1954, Tushinsky and his brother Irving founded Super-scope, Inc., to manufacture a film processing system they invented that converted old-fashioned "narrow film" for exhibition on the new CinemaScope wide screen. Despite some early promise—Walt Disney used the system for the reissue of *Fantasia*—Superscope never met with the success Tushinsky had expected. When the middle-aged Californian discovered Akio Morita's new stereophonic tape recorder, he found it easy to change his plans and drop the Superscope system in favor of the Japanese product.

On the surface, at least, this seemed to be a familiar pattern in Tushinsky's career. Many times in the past he had come close to grasping the brass ring, only to have it slip through his fingers. He played in Toscanini's orchestra, but only for a year; he started a light opera company that did well, but only for two seasons; he produced movies and screenplays, but never became really rich or famous in Hollywood. Now, with his wide screen invention failing to fulfill its early promise, he was starting over again in a new venture, selling a new product made by a small and unknown Japanese company.

But this time, things would be very different. Armed with the U.S. distribution rights to the Sony tape recorder (he had assigned the South American rights back to the company), Tushinsky built California-based Superscope, Inc., into a $200 million electronics importer. In one 10-year period—between 1967 and 1976—his importing business had a net income of $53.4 million, largely on the strength of the Sony product.

"Right from the start I knew that the Sony tape recorder couldn't miss in this country," he recalled. "Back in 1957, the public was looking for something new and advanced in electronics. The American companies weren't giving this to them, so the Japanese stepped in and filled the vacuum.

"The Sony tape recorder I brought here was the first Japanese import to make it in the American market. It paved the way for everything that followed, because it—along with the other Sony products—changed the image of 'made in Japan' from one of 'junk' to one of start-of-the-art technology."

That image didn't change overnight. Tushinsky had to fight the built-in bias that most Americans had toward things Japanese at a time when the memory of World War II was still fresh. He recalled the following incident: "My first year with Sony, I took the tape recorder to a trade show in New York, and it so happened that my booth was next to a couple of big American manufacturers. They laughed when they saw my display and told me I was crazy to think that I could sell that 'garbage' from Japan in this country. I said, 'Stop your laughing.' I knew that the Sony recorder would bury them. And, of course, it did."

Tushinsky overcame the prejudice against his Japanese product by running ads in electronics magazines, giving demonstrations of the tape recorder, and placing it in some of the biggest electronics dealers in the country. But what really won people over, according to the importer, was the Sony tape recorder's quality. "It was vastly superior to anything on the market. As more and more people became aware of this quality, our sales went through the roof."

With the demand for his Sony tape recorders growing, Tushinsky opened sales offices in New York, Chicago, and other cities. He also began importing audio and electronics products from other manufacturers in Japan and Taiwan.

At last it seemed that Joe Tushinsky had achieved the sort of really big success that had eluded him earlier in his career. But a little more than a decade after he had reached the agreement with Sony, a decision was made in Tokyo that threatened to bring his business crashing down. Tushinsky's original agreement with Sony entitled him to distribute tape recorders only. The Japanese company retained the U.S. distribution rights to all other products in its line, which over the years had grown to include a host of electronics goods, from televisions and radios to calculators and video cameras. In the early 1970s, Sony announced that it would be taking the U.S. distribution rights to its tape recorders away from Superscope and reassigning them to Sony Corporation of America, the subsidiary that sold its other products in this country.

After learning of Sony's decision, Tushinsky threatened to take the Japanese company to court. Wanting to avoid a legal battle, which was sure to create negative publicity for the company at a time when protectionist sentiment was beginning to surface in America, Sony reached an out-of-court settlement with Tushinsky that granted Superscope a final seven-year contract as its North American distributor of tape recorders.

Superscope's contract with Sony expired in December 1979. At this point, 69-year-old Joe Tushinsky could have walked away from his business and lived the comfortable life of a retired millionaire. But the short, barrel-chested Californian remained at Superscope and attempted to rebuild the company. ("What would I do if I retired?")

After reaching a post-Sony low in 1980, when it lost $13 million, the Chatsworth, California, firm (which now calls itself Marantz Co., Inc.), has been valiently trying to regain its profitability. By 1985, its annual deficit had been pruned to less than $1.6 million. Still the active head of the company, Joe Tushinsky has been pegging his hopes of a comeback on a line of products that includes stereo components, children's books and cassettes, and a high-tech version of the piano roll called the Pianocorder.

A computerized device mounted below the piano keyboard, the Pianocorder uses software cassettes to direct the instrument to "play" various compositions perfomed by artists like Vladimir Horowitz, Oscar Peterson, and Liberace.

"We have translated the performances of different artists into digital computer language and entered this into our software cassettes," explained Tushinsky. "When a cassette is put into the Pianocorder, it will instruct the piano's keys and pedals to operate in a manner that recreates the artist's performance. So, in effect, what you have is your piano playing a composition in the exact style that, say, Horowitz, would be playing if he were seated at that instrument."

Looking back on his career, how does Tushinsky feel about his Sony experience? "Listen, I'm not going to kid you, it still bothers me . . . sometimes. After all, I got involved with that company when it was almost nothing and I helped build it up.

"I even gave it the name Sony. Everybody there knew that they couldn't do a big export business with a name like Tokyo Tsushin, so they were looking for a substitute. They were going to use the name Sonny—S-O-N-N-Y—with a little boy trademark. I said, 'Come on, that's ridiculous.' At the time I was thinking of opening a branch office called Superscope of New York—so I suggested they take the initials from that—S-O-N-Y.

"I still say hello to Akio Morita when we run into each other at trade shows. A few years ago I saw him and he said to me, 'Joe-san'—they always called me Joe-san—'why are you still so upset, don't you realize we made you a millionaire?' 'Sure you made me a millionaire,' I said to him, 'but look what I made you. You're a multi-multi-millionaire. . . . '

"Still, I really don't have any complaints with the way things turned out. The Sony tape recorder was a product whose time had come back in the late '50s. Getting the rights to it when I did was obviously my big break."

6. Roy J. Carver had the rugged, lined face of a prairie settler, but the Iowa entrepreneur was an international traveler who owned a villa in Cannes, a 125-foot aluminum yacht, and a $2 million jet. Carver made his fortune from the Bandag tire
retreading process he discovered during a 1957 visit to Germany.

II

Upping
the Stakes

Jacob L. Barowsky (1892–1977)

ADELL CHEMICAL CO. (LESTOIL)

"Television showed us the way."

A compact, white-haired man who wore half-rim glasses and conservatively tailored suits, Jacob Barowsky looked more like the kindly grandfather he was than an advertising industry trend-setter. But in the mid-1950s, this Russian-born businessman, who was then in his sixties, engineered a marketing coup that permanently changed Madison Avenue's ideas about television advertising.

Barowsky was the president of Adell Chemical Co., a small but profitable Holyoke, Massachusetts, firm he started in 1933 at the age of 41 to make commercial cleaning compounds. Following World War II, he expanded into the retail market by introducing Lestoil, an all-purpose household cleaner. Lestoil was a marketing failure in its early years, never accounting for more than a small fraction of Adell's $500,000 volume. After trying unsuccessfully to pump some life into his ailing product with newspaper and radio ads, Barowsky turned to the new medium of television. As a small manufacturer with a limited ad budget, he could not afford to advertise on TV stations throughout his New England market unless he ran only a small number of spots in each city.

Barowsky rejected this idea, reasoning that television commercials had to be run frequently to create the necessary impact. With this in mind, he decided to concentrate all his advertising

47

in one city at a time, saturating that city with a barrage of commercials to establish a strong identity for Lestoil. After he had implemented this saturation campaign in one city, Barowsky planned to move on to the next town until he had covered all of New England. To ensure that his tight advertising budget would cover the cost of these campaigns, Barowsky planned to run commercials only during off-times (before 6 P.M. and after 11 P.M.), when the rates charged by stations were much lower. As an added cost-cutting step, he eliminated Lestoil's newspaper and radio advertising.

"Mr. Barowsky's primary concern was to get as many commercials as possible on TV in a given city," explained his son-in-law and former Adell vice-president, Isaac Eskenasy. "He didn't really care that his spots were run at off-times. His theory was that if you ran a spot on the Late Show every night for seven months, sooner or later everyone in town would see it. Plus, you'd get a small group of regular Late Show viewers who would become very familiar with your commercial message."

Jacob Barowsky could have walked into any office on Madison Avenue to learn why his advertising theories would never work. It was axiomatic in the ad industry that any TV campaign had to consist mainly, if not exclusively, of prime-time spots. What's more, no knowledgeable advertiser in the mid-1950s would have dared to limit himself exclusively to television and miss the millions of consumers who still did not own TV sets.

Luckily for Jacob Barowsky, he never consulted the experts. In February 1954, he began his advertising campaign by signing a $10,000 contract with local Holyoke station WHYN-TV to buy thirty off-time spots a week for the next year. Within months, Lestoil's sales increased sharply in the Holyoke market. Encouraged, Barowsky obtained a $75,000 line of credit from his local bank to finance saturation campaigns in Springfield, Massachusetts, and New Haven, Connecticut. This was followed, in 1955, by TV blitzes in Manchester, New Hampshire; Portland, Maine; Providence, Rhode Island; and other medium-sized New England cities. Surveys taken at the time showed that Lestoil was being used by up to 80 percent of the homemakers in markets where it was advertised.

Barowsky cracked his first big market, Boston, with a saturation campaign in March 1956. By the end of the year, sales of

7. An unlikely television advertising pioneer, Holyoke, Massachusetts, soap maker Jacob Barowsky was a 62-year-old grandfather in 1954 when he started advertising Lestoil on local station WHYN-TV. Barowsky's revolutionary strategy of saturating the market with early-morning and late-night TV spots flew in the face of the prevailing wisdom. (*Photo by Fabian Bachrach*)

household Lestoil had surpassed 1.7 million. Next came New York, where $400,000 was spent to run 123 TV spots per week. Philadelphia, Cleveland, Baltimore, Detroit, and other cities quickly fell into line as Lestoil advanced across the East and Midwest like a conquering army.

By 1958, sales of Lestoil had zoomed to $22 million, a 44,000 percent increase over the 1954 volume. Barowsky was buying $12.3 million worth of television time to advertise the household cleaner, making him the medium's biggest single-brand sponsor, ahead of such perennial giants as Coca-Cola. The sudden rise of Lestoil stunned the advertising industry, forcing it to take a new look at off-time television. Late night and early morning spots were no longer regarded as an exclusive domain of used car dealers and home improvement companies. Suddenly, television's biggest sponsors were complementing their network advertising with a liberal dosage of off-time commercials.

Lestoil's success also proved to be a boon to television's overall image with advertisers. Jacob Barowsky had gambled his entire budget on TV back in 1954, and his sales had soared. Newspapers and radio could not share the credit for this phenomenon; it clearly demonstrated the power of the new medium. Lestoil and Barowsky became the focus of considerable attention from the television and advertising industry trade press. Dozens of articles appeared describing Lestoil's "Four Fabulous TV Years."[1] The company also became the subject of a widely circulated sales film made by the Television Bureau of Advertising, entitled "The House That Television Built."

The creator of Lestoil never disputed his company's debt to television. Speaking before an advertising group in 1959, he said, "Television showed us the way—it is our first love and we will certainly continue to use it on a saturation basis wherever and whenever we possibly can." But Barowsky reminded his audience that Lestoil had also played a role in "building the house of television." He explained how his cleaning product's rapid growth had demonstrated the value of off-time spots, providing "a shot in the arm to the television industry [that] enabled them to sell in those time periods that heretofore went begging."[2]

Predictably, Lestoil's success inspired other manufacturers to introduce competing household cleaners, the most notable of which were Procter & Gamble's Mr. Clean and Lever Brothers' Handy Andy. Copying the advertising formula that Barowsky had used so effectively, his corporate competitors ran saturation campaigns on off-time television. Many of them also enlivened their commercials with jingles done in the style of Adell's famous theme song, "It's So Easy When You Use Lestoil."

Jacob Barowsky remained unruffled by his new competitors. "They're not the all-powerful giants everyone makes them out to be," he once said. "To me, size doesn't mean that much. A big company is a small company only with a lot of people, and a lot of bucks too."[3]

Ironically, Barowsky probably never would have gotten the chance to compete in the arena of big business were it not for a dispute with relatives in the 1930s over his plans to advertise the family's local chain of dry-cleaning stores. "Mr. Barowsky had an ongoing conflict with his brothers and a cousin about whether they should advertise their business. He was forever coming up with clever advertising ideas, which they would invariably oppose because they didn't want to spend the money," recalled Isaac Eskenasy. "Whenever he did advertise, sales would increase, but his relatives would always complain: 'You see, if you didn't waste all that money on advertising, we'd have even more profits now!'"

Eventually, this advertising dispute prompted Barowsky to leave the family business. "He became seriously ill in 1932 and had to have a kidney removed," said Eskenasy. "During his long convalescence, he thought about his situation a great deal, and then one day he told his wife, Adeline, 'I can't go back to dry cleaning; I've got to do something else.'"

What Barowsky wanted to do was create and market an entirely new product, a liquid detergent that worked equally well on water-soluble and insoluble stains. He knew from his career experience that once developed, such a detergent would find a ready market among dry cleaners and commercial launderers. Enlisting the aid of an employee from the family dry-cleaning business, John Tulenko, Barowsky mixed experimental batches of detergent in a baby's bathtub at his home. Less than one year later, he succeeded in developing a detergent that met all his requirements.

Barowsky introduced his liquid detergent to the dry-cleaning and laundry trade as Soap Solution in 1933. (The product's name was soon changed to Lavol and then, in 1936, to Lestoil.) The middle-aged entrepreneur broadened his customer base in the late 1930s by selling modified versions of his detergent to New England mills and factories. Looking to expand his market even further, Barowsky brought out household Lestoil for the retail shopper following World War II.

In 1960, Barowsky sold his detergent company to the conglomerate Standard International Corp. for more than $8 million. From that time until his death seventeen years later, he kept busy tending to other investments, traveling with his wife, enjoying his grandchildren and great-grandchildren, and involving himself in a wide range of civic causes.

It was a very good life, but one that had been tempered by adversity many times over the years. When Barowsky was six, his mother died, leaving him in the care of his stern and taciturn father, Abraham. The owner of a scrap metal yard, Abraham Barowsky saw little point in his son's education, and when Jacob was 14, he pulled the boy out of school, sending him to work at the family business without pay. Family, friends, and the Holyoke High School principal pressured the senior Barowsky for three years before he finally agreed to allow his son to return to school, provided the boy work at the scrap metal yard every morning from 5:30 until classes started. After being graduated from high school at 19, Jacob went on to attend Harvard, against his father's wishes, earning a degree in economics in 1915.

Following graduation, Jacob Barowsky experienced a long string of business reversals before starting the dry-cleaning chain with relatives in 1927. He had a paper jobbing firm that failed during the 1921 recession. He got involved in an unsuccessful metal products venture. He lost money in real estate in 1926, when the Florida land boom collapsed.

The most painful moment in Barowsky's life occurred in December 1956, when his 39-year-old-son, Seymour, died suddenly just as Lestoil was gaining real momentum. Once again, however, Jacob Barowsky found the strength to overcome misfortune. As they mourned the loss of their only son, he said to his wife, "We shall go on as if he were still with us."

When asked what lessons other entrepreneurs could learn from his father-in-law's career, Isaac Eskenasy responded without hesitation, "The importance of tenacity. In the 1950s, his son Seymour and I both left the company because we felt he was throwing money away advertising Lestoil instead of concentrating on the more profitable industrial products. He wished both of us luck and kept right on working—literally spending three dollars on advertising Lestoil for every dollar it made in sales. A couple of years later, Seymour and I returned to the company, because we had seen the potential of Lestoil—not because Mr. B. had changed his ideas about advertising. He knew he was right and he never wavered. That's the kind of man he was—very determined."

Roy J. Carver (1909–1981)

BANDAG, INC.

"Conceive, believe, achieve."

Not many people have heard of Bandag, Inc.—and no wonder. Located in the small Mississippi River town of Muscatine, Iowa, and concentrating on a single, unglamorous product sold to a specialized market, the company has never grabbed headlines with bold diversifications or bloody merger battles.

What Bandag does do is make money. Its annual revenues are consistently over $320 million, and its return on equity averaged 22 percent during the first half of the 1980s.

Virtually all of this wealth comes from a single source: truck tire retreading equipment and supplies, which Bandag manufactures and sells to a worldwide network of 1100 independent dealers. In 1986, Bandag's 500 U.S. dealers retreaded about six million truck tires, at over $100 per retread.

Bandag's quiet, low-keyed style provides a sharp contrast to the company's flamboyant, swashbuckling founder, the late Roy Carver. An imposing man, Carver looked like the kind of rugged pioneer who crossed the Iowa plains a century earlier, standing six-foot-five and weighing over 300 pounds, with a deeply lined face and long, flowing white hair brushed straight back.

Like his pioneering forebears, Carver was doggedly determined at everything he did, whether it involved working out a complex business problem or satisfying the whims of his palate. He once ordered a waiter to bring him some lemon, sugar, and water, and proceeded to stir up a fresh batch of lemonade in the middle of an elegant hotel dining room. On another occasion, he was visiting France when he developed a craving for Baskin-Robbins ice cream, so he had some flown in immediately from Muscatine.

An accomplished pilot himself, Carver acquired a reputation in Muscatine for his daredevil antics, once thrilling a crowd of townspeople by swooping under the old Muscatine High Bridge. The owner of a $2-million French-made Mustère jet, Carver often hopped in the 13-passenger craft and flew off to Europe or South America to visit Bandag dealers and suppliers.

The Bandag founder entertained international movie stars and celebrities either at his lavish villa in Cannes, France, or on board his Spanish-built yacht, a 125-foot aluminum craft that accommodated ten guests and seven crew members and had a landing pad for his six-passenger helicopter. For refreshment, guests were served Cuvée Roy James Carver, the Iowa centimillionaire's own private-label French wine.

Carver did not begin to amass his great fortune until relatively late in life, his ultimate success coming only after a long and hard struggle to overcome the technical difficulties involved in the application of his retread product.

The 47-year-old owner of a small, moderately successful industrial pump factory, Carver got into the tire retreading business in 1957 as a result of a chance discovery he made during a business trip to Germany. After attending a party in South Frankfurt, he was given a ride back to his hotel by another guest, a CIA agent whose car had an odd-looking set of retread tires. Unlike American retreads, in which the tread material extended all the way to the sidewalls, this tire's tread covered only the tire cap, the portion of the tire that actually comes into contact with the road. Carver's interest in the tires was further piqued when their owner gave a glowing account of their performance, claiming that they were far more durable than the originals.

The next day, Carver traveled to Darmstadt to visit Bernhard Nowak, the inventor of the retreading process. Nowak explained how his patented "Bandag" method worked: The tread pattern was pressed into a strip of rubber, which was then bonded to the tire with adhesive compounds under low pressure and temperature. This represented a radical departure from the conventional "hot cap" technique that relied on high temperatures and pressure to press the tread pattern onto the rubber strip as it was being attached to the tire. The heat and pressure used in hot cap retreading weakened the tire casing, making it less durable than Nowak's "cold retreads."

Convinced that Nowak's long-wearing retreads would find a ready market back in the U.S. among trucking companies and other high-volume tire users, Carver bought the North American rights to the inventor's Bandag process. In December 1957, he started Bandag, Inc. in Muscatine. When Bernhard Nowak died four years later, Carver acquired the worldwide rights to the retreading process from the German's estate.

Although Bandag's success would eventually propel Carver to the ranks of the super-rich, there was a period of time when it looked as if he had made the mistake of his life during that fateful trip to Germany. The retread tires that had been so effective on lightweight European passenger cars did not work nearly as well on American trucks, which, in addition to being much heavier, traveled over much greater distances, generating more tire heat. Under American road conditions, Bandag's rubber retread strip tended to peel off the tire, a problem that all but negated the demand for the product.

Roy Carver's friends and family urged him to forget about tire retreading and concentrate on his pump manufacturing business. But Carver was not the kind of person who was easily discouraged once he set his mind to achieving a goal.

Even as a teenager in rural Preemption, Illinois, he displayed an extraordinary degree of tenacity. After being told by his parents that they could not afford to support him while he attended high school in the city of Moline (Preemption had no school), the sophomore moved into the home of a local doctor and paid his own way by working alternately as a pharmacy clerk, a pinsetter at the YMCA bowling alley, and a laborer at the John Deere factory.

Carver graduated from high school on time with honors and won a scholarship to the University of Illinois, where he earned a degree in engineering. After working for awhile as a pump inspector for the state of Illinois, he started his own pump business on $100 capital in 1938. Operating out of a small workshop in the back of his brother's garage, Carver barely eked out a living until war orders in the early 1940s provided the volume he needed to get his business off the ground.

Having overcome tough obstacles in the past, Carver was confident that he could solve the difficulties that bedeviled Bandag. He hired a former B. F. Goodrich chemist named Ed Brodie and other industry experts to research new methods of joining retread strips to tires. As a college-trained engineer, Carver played an active role in this project, concentrating on developing advancements in the tread-making equipment, while Brodie worked on improving chemical adhesives.

To finance this extensive research, Carver dug deeply into the coffers of the Carver Pump Company, driving it close to the point of insolvency and angering its executives. At one point, the situation became so desperate that Carver had to raise $50,000 over the weekend so that the company could meet its expenses the following week. He did this by flying around the country and borrowing money from seven Bandag dealers. Some people in Muscatine like to say that Bandag might not exist today had bad weather prevented Carver from taking off that Friday. Others, who perhaps knew better, counter that no climatic inclemency could have kept the intrepid entrepreneur on the ground.

Harold Vischer, Bandag's retired executive vice-president and its first sales manager, is among the latter. "If Mr. Carver told me he was going to walk through a wall, and I really felt he believed he could do it, I would bet on his getting through the wall."

In 1964, after more than six years of dawn-to-dusk effort, Carver's research group broke through its wall and perfected a rubber retread strip that would not peel off the tire, even under the most extreme driving conditions.

The breakthrough involved three major developments. First, a new buffing unit was created that allowed tires to be "prepped" in an inflated, rather than deflated, position for greater accuracy. Second, Carver replaced the old metal curing bands that held the rubber strip in place during the bonding process with a flexible rubber envelope to achieve more uniform pressure. And, third, Brodie developed a superior uniform cushion gum material to use in place of the old binding cement.

Having surmounted this stumbling block, Carver still faced another, equally vexing, problem: how to overcome the negative image that Bandag had acquired during the early years, when it was plagued by peeling rubber strips. This task was made considerably more difficult by Bandag's steep price, which was about two times greater than the $20 cost of traditional hot cap retreads.

Carver overcame this problem by a combination of persistence and imaginative selling. When the owner of a large trucking fleet complained about Bandag's $40 price, Carver instructed his dealer to sell the man tires for $20, provided he agreed to pay an additional $20 every time Bandag equaled the life span of his previous retreads. Since Bandag typically lasted three, four, or even five times longer than other brands, the man ended up paying much more than the original $40. He also became a committed Bandag customer.

Years later, Carver would explain his decision to charge a premium price for his new product. "Had I elected to try to compete with the competition, to produce the cheapest and crummiest product, I would never have gotten the thing off the ground."

Once its application and image problems had been placed squarely behind it, Bandag not only got off the ground, it soared. The company's volume shot up at a dizzying rate: $3 million in 1964; $8 million in 1967; $70 million in 1973; $242 million in 1980.

Roy Carver, who had been ridiculed by established retreaders for his "nutty idea," suddenly found himself lionized as a pioneering genius. A *New York Times* article referred to Carver as "one of the wealthiest and cleverest businessmen in Iowa"[1]; President Johnson presented his company with the Presidential "E" Award for Excellence in exporting; and the National Tire Dealers and Retreaders Association elected him into the Tire Industry Hall of Fame.

Still, this notoriety and fortune was not without its costs. Roy Carver had, by most accounts, some trouble making the emotional transition from a moderately prosperous but obscure Iowa businessman to a nationally recognized captain of industry. Always a peripatetic man, Carver began spending even more time away from his Muscatine home, a practice that understandably strained his relations with his second wife, Lucille, his adult children, and some of his old friends.

Eventually, however, Carver seemed to settle down. He sold his French villa and began spending more time in his hometown.

He also increased his already considerable charitable activities, the main beneficiary of which was the University of Iowa. Among his gifts to the school were a $3.7 million contribution to build a major addition to the university's hospital (the Roy J. Carver Pavilion); funds to underwrite a professorship in internal medicine; a gallery addition to the museum of art; artificial turf for the football stadium; and $2 million for the construction of the Carver-Hawkeye Sports Arena.

Carver's most consuming interest at the school, however, was its wrestling team, a perennial NCAA champion. He very seldom missed an Iowa wrestling meet; on those rare occasions when he could not attend, he sent his secretary, who telephoned him with the results as soon as the match was over regardless of where he was in the world.

A frequent visitor to the Iowa locker room, Carver liked to inspire Hawkeye wrestlers with pep talks built around his personal "Conceive, believe, achieve" philosophy. The team, in turn, adopted Carver's motto as its own.

In his later years, the Bandag founder became involved in other business activities, not all of them successful. He lost $17 million in a Mideast oil drilling investment, which ended with Carver suing his partner for misrepresentation in 1980.[2]

One year later, Carver died of a heart attack in Marbella, Spain. At his funeral, a Kipling poem was read: "If you can trust yourself when all men doubt you. . . . " It was an appropriate eulogy for a man who, at mid-life, had spent over six years laboring on a project that few believed had any chance of succeeding.

John K. Hanson (1913–)

WINNEBAGO INDUSTRIES, INC.

"Learning the lessons of small business."

Forest City is a quiet, unassuming community, even by Iowa standards. Tucked away near the northern border of the state, its business district consists of a three-block row of glass-paned brick storefronts, where merchants sell clothing and other necessities to farmers from surrounding Winnebago County.

Daily life hadn't changed much in this rural trading outpost since it was founded in 1855. So when *Time* magazine came out to do a story on one of its citizens in 1947, everyone in Forest City took notice. The subject of the story was John K. Hanson, a furniture and appliance dealer, who had dreamed up a clever gimmick for drawing farmers to his store. In lieu of cash, Hanson was accepting livestock and produce as payment for couches, refrigerators, and washers. The spectacle of wagonloads of hogs and corn lined up in front of his Clark Street store was seen in the December 19, 1947, issue of *Time* by readers across the country.

Its one moment in the national limelight notwithstanding, Forest City followed the downhill course typical of small midwestern towns after World War II. Farming had become less profitable, driving younger residents away to places like Waterloo and Cedar Rapids to seek factory work. Concerned that their city would become a ghost town, a group of Forest City businessmen

59

8. John Hanson's offer to trade refrigerators and ovens for hogs and cattle was a major success for his combination appliance-furniture store.

joined together in the late 1950s to draw outside industry, and jobs, to the community.

It was only natural that the group turn for leadership to their local celebrity, John K. Hanson. "John K."—in addition to the furniture store—had run an International Harvester dealership and, having become Iowa's youngest licensed embalmer in his early twenties, owned the town's funeral parlor. Now 44, burly and balding, he was regarded as a skillful promoter who could work whatever miracles it would take to save Forest City.

Hanson wouldn't let his fellow townspeople down. Over the next decade, the waning Iowa community would undergo a transformation that would prompt one local woman to exclaim, "If I was on the other side of the U.S., I would think it was the wildest story I ever heard." The town's population would double to nearly 5000, hundreds of Forest Citians would see their net worth increase by sums ranging from $10,000 to $100,000 and more, and two dozen of them—including a newspaperman, a dentist, and a contractor—would become millionaires. John K. himself would be ranked as one of the 400 wealthiest individuals in America[1]: the founder and principal stockholder in Winnebago

Industries, the nation's number one manufacturer of recreational vehicles.

Ironically, it was a story in *Time* on a trailer and camping boom in California that first got Hanson thinking in terms of starting a recreational vehicle (RV) plant in Forest City. He traveled west to check out the situation for himself, and returned with enough enthusiasm to convince 209 locals to put up a total of $50,000 to form a company to build travel trailers for a Gardena, California, manufacturer.

Plagued by management disputes from the start, the venture failed, going bankrupt just months after the first Forest City–made trailer rolled off the production line in March 1958. But Hanson remained convinced that there was money to be made in RVs. "Trends move from West to East," he later explained. "I'd seen how big they were in California, and I knew it was only a matter of time before they'd be sweeping the rest of the country."

He bought out the other investors for a few thousand dollars and assumed control of the plant and its inventory. Although he had been planning on retiring in a few years, once circumstances thrust him into the RV business he was determined to see the venture through. Like himself, his father and grandfathers had been prairie entrepreneurs, wily midwesterners who hustled in and out of cattle, crops, and dealerships, learning to move quickly and follow their instincts. Not the kind of men to let an opportunity pass by.

Hanson insists that his early experience as a small-town businessman provided ideal training for building Winnebago into a national corporation. "If you want to learn about business, for heaven's sake don't go to a big concern. It is too specialized. I tell the young men to go to a small one where they can learn about trades, terms, notes, contracts, parts and pieces, installation, repairs."

For Hanson, this educational process began during high school, when, at the insistence of his father, he worked a different job every year. "I didn't like it a bit," he recalled, "because I coulda made more money if I stayed in one place."

Looking back, however, he concedes the idea had merit, exposing him to a wide variety of businesses and business practices. One of the most valuable lessons he learned came while he was working at a clothing store and involved what Hanson terms

9. The Forest City, Iowa, businessman used skills as a promoter to build Winnebago into the world's largest mobile home company. Hanson was 45 when he founded Winnebago in 1958 out of the ruins of a failed trailer manufacturing venture.

"merchandising." His employer purchased a gross of neckties for Christmas at 50¢ and 70¢ apiece, and marked them up to 59¢ and 79¢. But then the store owner did a strange thing; he placed some of the better ties into a third group with a 99¢ price tag. It was the latter neckties, to teenaged John K.'s astonishment, that sold out the fastest.

"It's all a matter of merchandising—finding what people are willing to spend. In this case, they wanted to pay a dollar for a necktie for Christmas," he pointed out. "So you charge people more money, give them more quality—or at least the image of quality—and take more margin for yourself. That's merchandising."

This principle was applied effectively at Winnebago Industries thirty years later. By making some RV models available with deluxe trimmings, such as larger windows, more luxurious upholstery and drapery fabrics, and stove hoods with power vents, the trailer manufacturer was able to realize a greater profit margin. "If you spend an extra fifty bucks—put on a little chrome, a little paint—you can get five hundred for it," Hanson advised. "General Motors does it all the time."

By 1969 Hanson was marketing twenty models of trailers, pickup campers, and motor homes with such amenities as bathtubs and his-and-hers closets. His company was growing four times as fast as the RV industry, which was itself exploding at a rate of 25 percent a year!

An early sell-up feature was Winnebago's use of foam rubber cushions and mattresses in place of the heavier spring-filled furniture then found in RVs. As a former furniture dealer, Hanson knew that foam rubber was a premium product that could command a higher retail price. To further enhance his bottom line, he began manufacturing his own foam cushions and mattresses in the basement of what had been Hanson's Furniture Store. "Why should we give a supplier a profit, when we can make a profit?" was his reasoning. Vertical integration at Winnebago eventually reached the point where the company was making virtually everything it used on its RVs, with the exception of the appliances and Dodge chassis.

Of all his manufacturing innovations, Hanson is most proud of the "unbalanced panel" now used in the assembly of vehicle roofs, floors, and sidewalls. The laminated panel consists of plywood on the inside, aluminum on the outside, and a layer of styrofoam insulation sandwiched in between. When it was developed in 1963, it offered the advantages of being lighter and less expensive to produce than the "balanced" metal-foam-metal panels then being used by other trailer manufacturers, enabling Winnebago to sell, in Hanson's words, "a better product at a lower price."

By 1965, Winnebago's annual sales had surpassed $2.8 million, and the company made its first offering of common stock: 24,000 shares at an issue price of $12.50 per share. Five years later, it became the first corporation deriving most of its revenues from RV sales to be listed on the New York Stock Exchange.

Among those who purchased Winnebago stock were 1000 Forest Citians, more than one-fifth of the rural community's residents. Farmers, secretaries, schoolteachers—cautious Iowans who had never played the stock market before—emptied their savings accounts of $100, $500, and $1000 to buy a piece of the local factory.

Their hometown pride and faith in John K. was rewarded. In 1971, Winnebago, up 462 percent, was the biggest gainer on the New York Stock Exchange. A $1000 investment made six years earlier, when the company first went public, was worth a million dollars. Stores all along the city's three-block business district began posting the day's selling price of Winnebago in their windows—42½, 60, 84. Like the boom towns of the Gold Rush era, Forest City had struck it rich.

How did the prairie investors react to their sudden fortune? "Some did good, some did bad," said Hanson. "It's like winning at poker, some cash in their chips and put it in the bank, and some of 'em play 'til they lose it all." There were lifelong farmers who indulged in conspicuous displays of wealth, building homes with indoor swimming pools; others were content to limit their spending to a new Singer sewing machine.

Then in the mid-1970s, Forest City's gold mine threatened to run dry. The fuel crisis hit, causing the bottom to drop out of the RV market. To make matters worse, Winnebago's management had grown complacent. Hanson had semi-retired in 1977, handing over the firm's presidency to his son John V., and his innovative leadership was sorely missed. While its competitors were introducing trimmer, more fuel-efficient motor homes, the Iowa manufacturer was marketing lumbering gas guzzlers basically unchanged from a decade earlier.

Winnebago's stock dropped to an all-time low of $1.75 in 1979. The following year the company lost $13.5 million and slipped to third place in the industry, behind Coachman and Fleetwood.

Unable to watch from the sidelines any longer, 65-year-old John K. Hanson came out of retirement and resumed control. His first, widely publicized move was to shake up the company's management, replacing his son with former operations vice-president Ron Haugen as president of the firm. Next, Hanson embarked on a round of belt tightening, slashing Winnebago's payroll from 4000 to 800 employees and closing two production facilities. "I came in like Wyatt Earp. I just lined 'em up and shot 'em down," he later recounted.

But Winnebago's ultimate survival hinged on its ability to update its product line by developing new vehicles aimed at a mileage-conscious public, and it was here that Hanson focused most of his attention. Within three years the company introduced two downsized, aerodynamically styled motor homes. These were powered by front-wheel-drive Renault diesel engines, which got 22-plus miles per gallon and proved to be a substantial improvement over the previous 8 to 12 mpg.

By 1984, thanks to good public reception of the new Winnebagos and a general recovery in the RV market, the company was back in the black and once again the industry leader. Also back was the younger Hanson, who, his father now insists, wasn't fired at all, but left and subsequently returned on his own volition. "When they're young, they don't think their mommies and daddies know anything," Hanson said, shrugging off the boardroom dispute. "But when they get a little older, they start seeing things differently."

Aging has its advantages in other areas too; namely, in the increased business acumen it brings, Hanson believes. Asked if he felt he could have started a company the magnitude of Winnebago while in his twenties or thirties, he snapped in his lion's growl, "Impossible. Not enough knowledge, experience. It would have been an absolute no-no."

David Mintz *(1931–)*

TOFUTTI BRANDS, INC.

"A little voice kept whispering, 'Keep going'."

His neighbors said he was crazy. The experts he consulted told him he was wasting his time. His wife thought he had become obsessed. But David Mintz persisted, filling the night with the sound of clattering pots and high-pitched mixers, as he looked for a way to make a nondairy frozen dessert from the fermented soybean curd, tofu.

That was in the late 1970s. A few years later, the result of Mintz's incessant experimentation would sweep the nation as Tofutti, a pleasant-tasting frozen dessert with no cholesterol, no butterfat, and only about one-third the calories of premium ice cream. Tofutti is now the flagship product of Tofutti Brands, Inc., a $17 million Rahway, New Jersey, company headed by Mintz.

A likable Brooklyn native, David Mintz began experimenting with tofu in the early 1970s, seeking a nondairy substitute to use at his kosher delicatessen. "If you keep kosher, you can't mix meat and dairy, okay?" he said in the rapid-fire delivery of a Catskills comic. "But I wanted to serve my customers things like beef stroganoff and lasagna, so I was always looking for something to use in place of dairy. But everything I ever tried tasted just awful."

Then one day Mintz read an article in a health and nutrition magazine about tofu. A gelatin-like soybean curd, tofu had long been used in Asian cuisine, but was just beginning to gain acceptance among health-conscious Americans who used it as a cholesterol- and lactose-free dairy substitute.

"After a read that article I said, 'Hey, wait a minute, this is what I've been looking for all my life.' So I went to Chinatown, picked up a pail of tofu and started experimenting."

Mintz's early experiments yielded impressive results. "The first thing I made was tofu 'sour cream' for my stroganoff. That was pretty easy; I put the tofu in a blender, threw in some lemon juice, added a little seasoning, a touch of mustard, and boom— I had sour cream. Then I started to make tofu pancakes, tofu cheese dips, tofu quiche. . . . It was fantastic. Discovering tofu was like discovering America; it opened a whole new world."

Tofu proved to be such a realistic substitute for dairy products that some of Mintz's customers suspected him of violating kosher law. One woman yelled at him, "Have you lost your religion?" Other customers threw down their napkins and vowed never to return to his delicatessen. A few nonkosher patrons gave him knowing winks, "This is just like the stroganoff I make at home." Eventually Mintz had to tack up posters explaining, "What Is Tofu?"

10. Brooklyn delicatessen owner David Mintz was looking for a dairy substitute to use in dishes at his kosher restaurant in the 1970s when he found out about tofu. His constant experiments eventually led to the creation of a frozen dessert that he called Tofutti.

The delicatessen owner soon became known throughout his neighborhood as a wizard of tofu cookery, his reputation boosted by talks given at the local Weight Watchers chapter. "I was getting a little heavy, so I joined Weight Watchers," he recounted. "At the meetings, I would mention how I was cutting calories by us- ing tofu instead of dairy. Before long I was getting calls from people who wanted my recipes. So I started to lecture at Weight Watchers on the benefits of tofu."

Despite his success at duplicating traditional dairy-based en- trees, Mintz had a difficult time trying to develop a tofu ice cream substitute. Tofu's soybean flavor, never noticeable in a heavily spiced and cooked dish like stroganoff, dominated the more sub- tle-tasting ingredients in frozen desserts. And the gelatin texture, which broke down when tofu was cooked, became inconsistent and objectionable when frozen.

"Dessert was a whole different ball game," recalled Mintz. "No matter what I did, I couldn't get the results I wanted. I tried add- ing eggs and cooking the tofu, I tried doing everything, but noth- ing worked. I became obsessed with finding a tofu dessert. Ideas would come to me in the middle of the night, and I'd jump out of bed and hurry to the kitchen to try them. My wife was con- vinced that I had flipped out, and really, she might have been right; tofu had become a thing with me."

Finally, Mintz visited a university to discuss his problem with food technologists. "They told me to forget it, that the idea of a soy-based dessert had been tried before and it just couldn't be done. This only made me want to do it more. A little voice inside my head kept whispering, 'Keep going, keep going.' So I made up my mind not to listen to the 'experts.' The biggest obstacle to anyone's success are the people who will tell him it can't work."

By the end of the 1970s, Mintz had finally succeeded in cre- ating a frozen tofu dessert that had an agreeable soy-free taste and the smooth texture of ice milk and frozen yogurt. Without divulging any trade secrets, the Tofutti inventor did offer some insights into the tofu dessert-making process.

"Every Tofutti flavor represented a different challenge, and each one was hard to get right. The toughest flavor was probably strawberry. Most people don't realize this, but the strawberry has a very delicate taste. When I mixed strawberries with tofu, the soy flavor would overpower them, and no matter how many strawberries I put in, it would still come out tasting like soy. Then I finally discovered that I could bring out the taste of strawberries, and kill the taste of soy, by adding apple juice."

Having perfected his frozen dessert formula, Mintz test-marketed it in 1979 by giving free samples to patrons at his delicatessen on Third Avenue in Manhattan. When people began asking where they could buy the product, the restaurateur set up a freezer display of vanilla, chocolate, and strawberry packages near his register counter. Once he started to package his product, Mintz had to give it a name: "Tofutti just came to me late one night, and I knew it was right."

Soon the demand for Tofutti spread beyond Manhattan. "We were getting calls from all over New York, New Jersey, and Connecticut," said Mintz. "People would say, 'My daughter was at your restaurant last week, and she said you have this product that tastes like ice cream but doesn't have cholesterol. Well, I'm on a low-cholesterol diet—where can I buy some?' "

By 1981, it was clear that Mintz faced a major decision: he could remain at his restaurant and sell Tofutti as a sideline, or he could leave the security of his established delicatessen-catering business and risk everything in an attempt to turn his invention into a national food product. Once again, the little voice inside David Mintz's head gave him the answer—"Do it!"

"I was 50 years old, and I had a successful delicatessen and catering business that employed over 60 people, but I sold everything and started over again. A lot of people said I must have gone crazy to do this at 50. But I told them, 'Look, for my first 50 years I owned a deli, for my next 50 I'm going to make Tofutti.' "

Mintz purchased an abandoned frozen food warehouse in Brooklyn, primarily because it was inexpensive and had freezer walls already in place. He spent the next year working alone to repair the run-down building. Recently divorced (he has since remarried), he moved from his comfortable Manhattan apartment to more modest quarters in Sheepshead Bay, Brooklyn.

"It got to the point where I said to myself, 'Why should I be living in luxury, when I'm roughing it in business?' So I left my beautiful apartment for a little run-down place. But I loved it. I was on my own breaking new ground. I really think I felt like the people in the covered wagons must have felt when they went out west."

Mintz sold his first order of Tofutti to a shop called The Health Nut in Manhattan. "I delivered it myself in my car, and I wound up getting a $45 ticket for double parking when I dropped the order off, but I didn't care—my business was on its way."

Initially, Mintz marketed Tofutti primarily to health food stores in New York. His first big break occurred when Bloomingdale's placed an order, giving Tofutti exposure to a large number of shoppers. "Then we started getting orders from all over the place," said Mintz. "To give you an idea of how fast we grew, I started out alone with one phone and an answering machine; within a year or two, my office had thirty-eight phones that were ringing like crazy."

In December 1983, Mintz took his growing company public. Its stock opened at 5¾ a share; six months later the price had jumped to over $12 a share. To keep up with the increasing national demand for his product, Mintz began contracting Tofutti production out to independent dairies. Then, in 1985, he moved the company from Brooklyn to a more spacious, modern facility in Rahway.

"Not only do we have a bigger building in New Jersey, we also have more loading docks and better access to the interstates, so it's easier to truck our products to stores all over the country," he said. "I even moved to New Jersey myself, and it's beautiful. We have a lot of trees and open spaces; it's like being out in the country."

The "countryside" of New Jersey is indeed a long way from the Williamsburg section of Brooklyn where David Mintz was raised. The son of a struggling baker, Mintz remembers his boyhood ambition was "to become rich." He thought that the surest way to do this was in the fur business. "When I graduated from high school, people who sold furs made more than doctors."

But the fur trade did not provide the expected riches, and in 1965 Mintz moved to the Catskills, where he opened a small grocery store in the town of Mountaindale. Exhibiting the business acumen that would later serve him well as a manufacturer, the 24-year-old grocer soon realized that there was more profit in selling prepared foods than there was in groceries.

"I started selling fried chicken from a little counter in my store, and this went over very well," he recalled. "Then I added knishes and stuffed cabbage, and I had lines outside my store."

Encouraged by this success, Mintz opened a delicatessen in the bigger Catskills town of Monticello. He advertised for kitchen help with a classified ad headlined: "Grandmothers Wanted." Response to the ad was overwhelming. "All of these adorable little grandmothers came out of the woodwork, and I hired them to make their specialties for my deli," he recalled. "A lot of them didn't want their families to know that they were working, so they'd say, 'I can only come in between two and four when my daughter goes shopping, but I make a wonderful kugel.' They liked the idea of working, because it made them feel useful. Much of what I know about food came from these wonderful ladies."

Mintz then opened a delicatessen in Brighton Beach, followed by a bigger location on Church Avenue in Brooklyn and a third restaurant in Manhattan. By the early 1970s, he had sold his Catskills locations to concentrate on his city restaurants and an expanding catering service.

"I was really doing quite well in the restaurant and catering business by the time Tofutti came along," he said. "I could have finished out my career in comfort there, but this was not for me. I wanted the challenge."

Chairman and CEO of Tofutti Brands, Inc., Mintz has turned down several buyout offers from larger corporations. "Our attitude is, 'Thanks, but no thanks.' There are still a lot of things that we want to do at Tofutti. We are just beginning to scratch the surface of what can be done with soy."

Among the plans that Mintz has on the drawing board are tofu cookies and pastries and soy meatballs. "Once again, I have people telling me that my ideas for new soy products won't work," said the Tofutti inventor. But David Mintz just smiles and shrugs off the skeptics, and the little voice inside his head still whispers, "Keep going, keep going."

11. Comedian Jerry Lewis entertains Perry Mendel and children at a Kinder-Care center. The child care company made the Muscular Dystrophy Association its national charity in 1978, and since that time has raised well over $1 million for MDA.

III

Riding a Wave

Perry Mendel (1922–)

KINDER-CARE LEARNING CENTERS, INC.

"An idea will remain just an idea until someone moves on it."

Perry Mendel has often been described as the "Colonel Sanders of the child care industry," and, indeed, the genial Kinder-Care chairman has a great deal in common with the late Kentucky Fried Chicken founder. Like the legendary colonel, Mendel is a southerner who speaks with the thumping enthusiasm of a country preacher, but whose sharp, analytical mind would be right at home on Wall Street.

Even Mendel's Kinder-Care centers, with their peaked bright red roofs, bear a physical resemblance to the Colonel's Kentucky Fried Chicken restaurants. They are almost as commonplace, too: in 1985 the silver-haired entrepreneur had 1050 centers operating in forty states and Canada, making Kinder-Care the clear leader in the multi-billion-dollar child care industry.

But unlike Colonel Sanders, whose company pioneered the fast food chicken restaurant, Perry Mendel was not the originator of the idea for a standardized child care chain. In fact, he was inspired to start Kinder-Care in the 1960s, after reading an article in the now-defunct *National Observer* about a large franchise company's plans to enter the child care business.

"I have always been a real reader and a follower of business trends," said Mendel. "If you'll recall, back in the 1960s, newspapers and magazines were filled with articles about women entering the work force and the growing demand for day-care facilities that this was creating. Looking around in my hometown of Montgomery, Alabama, I began to suspect that there was a real need for child care centers that offered something more than the substandard custodial care that children were receiving at the independent centers people ran out of their homes."

Then Mendel read the *National Observer* article that described how Performance Systems, a Nashville franchise company, was considering developing a chain of child care centers. The article gave a glowing description of the proposed chain's potential, complete with projections for the continued growth of the child care market. This, said Perry Mendel, was "the clincher" that convinced him to start Kinder-Care.

"After I read that article, I did my own pro forma, and the numbers looked very good. I wasn't the first to come up with the idea for a child care chain, but I wanted to be the first to make it work. An idea will remain just an idea until someone moves on it, and that's what Kinder-Care did. We were the first to turn the idea of a national child care chain into a reality."

Achieving this feat was not easy for Mendel, who was 46 when he opened the first Kinder-Care center on July 14, 1969, in Montgomery. Though large, the child care market proved to be far more resistant to the chain concept than the *National Observer* article had indicated. (Performance Systems had become so frustrated with its child care business that it dropped out of the industry in the early 1970s.)

In trying to establish a profitable child care chain, Mendel and other entrepreneurs faced a unique set of problems. A child care center is a very labor-intensive operation, requiring one teacher for every five to ten children. This, coupled with the fact that a single center can accommodate only a limited number of children without sacrificing the quality of its service, means extremely low profit margins. An entrepreneur who hoped to prosper would have to compensate for these low margins by attracting a high volume of customers. To do this, he or she would have to open many locations in a relatively short time.

The logical way to achieve this goal would be to franchise centers to independent investor-operators. Entrepreneurs in other low margin–high volume industries had been successfully expanding through franchising since the 1950s, but, as Kinder-Care and others in the child care industry were soon to discover,

caring for children was a far more demanding business than selling hamburgers—and one that required much closer supervi-
sion. Child care companies that attempted to grow through franchising soon found themselves unable to maintain their quality
standards.

"We tried to go the franchising route at first, but it didn't
work out," recalled Mendel. "The people who bought franchises,
often ex-teachers or ex-ministers, thought they would love to work
with children, but most of them didn't know a thing about getting a building into existence or financing. We wound up having
to handle all of the details for them, and even then we had no
real control over how well they conformed to the standards we
established for a Kinder-Care center."

After seven months in business, Mendel got out of franchising. Today, he calls this "the best corporate decision we ever
made," explaining that company-owned centers give Kinder-Care
greater control over the quality of its service and a better return
on its investment.

Back in the winter of 1970, however, Mendel had good reason
to second-guess his decision to stop franchising. A public stock
offering had failed to produce the capital needed to finance the
opening of more than a handful of company-owned centers, leaving Kinder-Care with a volume that was too low to yield significant corporate profits.

By July, Kinder-Care had fewer than twenty centers grossing
about $12,000 a week, and Mendel was ready to scale down his
dream of a nationwide child care chain. "One day I was going
to lunch with a young tax attorney I had just brought into the
company named Dick Grassgreen—who, by the way, is now my
president—and I said to him, 'Dick, if we can't get this company
up to the point where we think it should be soon, then I guess
you can always go back to practicing law. As for me, I'll operate
the few centers we have as a small business.'

"I knew that what we had with Kinder-Care was good," continued Mendel. "We just needed much more of it if we were going
to get off the ground as a corporation. If we couldn't finance our
growth through the sale of stock, we would have to consider
merging with someone bigger than us."

Reluctantly, Mendel merged Kinder-Care with Warner National, a Cincinnati real estate firm, in late 1970. The $1.5 million

he received from Warner allowed him to open a few new centers and expand Kinder-Care's services beyond its initial program for 2½-to-6-year-old children to include infant and after-school programs.

But Kinder-Care's real growth did not begin until a year later, when Mendel developed a real estate financing plan that offered all the benefits of franchising without the drawbacks. The plan worked this way: an outside investor would build a child care center to Mendel's specifications and then lease it to Kinder-Care for 20 years with two 5-year options to renew. The investors would thus be financing Kinder-Care's expansion, but at the same time Mendel would be able to maintain tight control over the operation of each new center.

Everyone came out ahead under Mendel's plan. The investor, who typically put up $50,000 on a $150,000 mortgage, received a guaranteed $24,000-a-year lease income from Kinder-Care. Even allowing for interest charges, this netted him about $7500, a 15 percent pretax return on his investment. For its part, Kinder-Care was able to open new company-owned centers without incurring building costs.

"We often got into a building with just the investment in equipment—about $10,000 or $15,000," said Mendel. "One of the keys to our early success was our ability to implement a sophisticated real estate financing plan."

Using this plan to attract investors, Mendel opened new Kinder-Care centers almost as fast as they could be built. The number of centers, which stood at 17 at the end of 1970, jumped to 88 in 1975 and 133 in 1976, the year Mendel reacquired complete control of his company from Warner National. By the end of the decade, Kinder-Care—which was, in its founder's words, "practically insolvent" 10 years earlier—had 335 child care centers producing over $28.5 million in operating revenues and $2.2 million in net earnings.

As his company grew, Perry Mendel turned his attention to assembling a team of talented managers and child care specialists. "My original idea was to take the guilt away from mothers who had to leave their children in a child care facility by offering them a comprehensive child care program in a safe, clean, colorful, and happy environment," he said. "I hired the best experts I could find to develop programs in nutrition, education, and muscle coordination, all with the idea of providing the child with something much more than custodial care.

"Right from the start, we sold our service on quality rather than price. We were charging $20 per week in 1969, when the going price for child care in Montgomery was $13 to $15. But we were the first to give the child a hot breakfast."

Like all companies in the child care industry, Kinder-Care's biggest problem is keeping qualified teachers. Because rendering child care is a labor-intensive activity, Kinder-Care and its competitors pay their teachers at or near the minimum wage level. This has led to a turnover rate that has been described as being "the equivalent of a fast food operation."[1]

Kinder-Care has managed to control its turnover rate, however, by adopting a promote-from-within policy that gives teachers the opportunity to advance to manager and district manager positions, and by offering an employee stock plan that awards shares in the company to every employee over 21 years of age who has completed three years of uninterrupted service. Another morale booster is the Kinder-Care *Centerline,* a monthly publication for teachers filled with company news, photos, and inspirational messages ("You Are the Hub of Our Company").

Perry Mendel recalled how Kinder-Care's house organ was inspired by his own work experience. "When I was a young man, I worked at an Edison Brothers shoe store in Atlanta. Edison Brothers was a very sharp company out of St. Louis, and I learned a lot about merchandising from them. One of the things they taught me was how important it is to have a company publication when you have stores scattered over a wide area of the country. You cannot possibly get out and visit all of those stores, so the only way to maintain contact with the people who are out there on the front line, so to speak, is through a magazine. I remember how much I looked forward to receiving the Edison Brothers magazine every month, and I've tried to duplicate this feeling with our publication here at Kinder-Care."

The Edison Brothers job was not the only, nor the most important, past experience that Perry Mendel drew on to build his child care chain. Born in Atlanta to a restaurateur father, Mendel was involved in several small business ventures before Kinder-Care, including an auto parts store, a chemical factory, and a real estate company that specialized in developing shopping centers.

Mendel's experience at the real estate firm, which he operated with his three brothers-in-law, played an especially important role in the development of Kinder-Care. The real estate
financing plan that he used to fuel the rapid spread of Kinder-
Care centers in the mid-1970s was modeled on a similar plan the
partners had used to raise capital for shopping center construction.

"My years of experience in real estate gave me a tremendous
advantage when I started Kinder-Care," acknowledged Mendel.
"The expertise that our company had in real estate and financing
allowed us to grow quickly and get a big jump on the competition."

The Kinder-Care founder said that the success of his company has not wrought any great changes in his life. ("Success is
a humbling experience; it should not change what you are.") A
fit and vigorous 64-year-old who frequently puts in 10-hour days
at the office, Mendel has no intention of retiring from the chairmanship of his $235 million company.

"So long as the good Lord grants me good health, I will be
at Kinder-Care. I see tremendous opportunities for us to grow
in new directions in the future."

Indeed, throughout the history of Kinder-Care, Mendel has
pushed the company into new and profitable areas. He formed
Kinder-Care Merchandise, Inc., to sell emblematic shirts, caps,
bibs, jackets, and other items; Kinder Life, to market life insurance for children; and Kindustry, to operate child care centers
at corporate facilities for clients like Campbell Soup Co. and the
Equitable Life Assurance Society.

The phenomenal success of Kinder-Care has raised disturbing questions in the minds of some critics, who have used epi-
thets like "Kentucky Fried Children" to deride the highly standardized child-care-for-profit centers.

Perry Mendel remains unflustered by this criticism. "We made
affordable to middle-income America what had previously been
affordable only to upper-income America: clean, safe, enriching
child care that goes well beyond the custodial level."

Writing about Kinder-Care in an article for the June 5, 1977,
New York Times Sunday magazine, Joseph Lelyveld asked, "Does
it sound a little mercenary? I suppose it does, but the idea that

parents and children are consumers is also a little refreshing. It implies they are entitled to choices and their money's worth."[2]

And, even as the company's most strident critics are forced to acknowledge, Perry Mendel's Kinder-Care centers are light-years ahead of the makeshift child care facilities they replaced.

William H. Millard (1932–)

COMPUTERLAND CORP.

"Anybody ... had the opportunity to observe this phenomenon."

Few people in the history of American business have made and lost as much money in as short a time as William Millard.

In 1975, Millard was the owner of a small, near-bankrupt personal computer company. One year later, he founded ComputerLand, the phenomenally successful franchised chain of retail computer stores. The middle-aged California entrepreneur became one of the wealthiest men in the country as a result of ComputerLand's growth, his personal fortune soaring to $500 million in 1983 and $600 million in 1984.[1]

But then Millard's fortunes declined even more rapidly than they had once risen. A successful lawsuit initiated by a former ComputerLand employee stripped Millard of 20 percent of his privately held company and forced him to pay over $141 million in punitive damages and fees in the spring of 1985. This, together with a sharp dip in ComputerLand's performance and the threat of rebellion on the part of its franchisees, caused Millard's fortune to fall by more than 60 percent in two years, leaving him with a net worth estimated at $200 million in 1986.

Coincidental with this loss of wealth was a loss of power, which was for the fiercely independent Millard even more devastating. Under pressure from his new "partners" following the lawsuit, Millard resigned as chairman and chief executive of ComputerLand in the fall of 1986 and retreated with his family to the Pacific island of Saipan. At last report, he intended to sell his remaining interest in ComputerLand and start a utility company to power the Mariana Islands.

Ironically, the same strong-willed intensity that propelled William Millard to the pinnacle of success was also responsible for his sudden and dramatic decline.

"He is an extremely determined, visionary entrepreneur," Norman Dinnsen, one of the earliest and most successful ComputerLand franchisees, told the authors of this book.

This determination and vision allowed Millard to overcome repeated business reversals and pioneer the concept of the computer retailing center. However, as Dinnsen also pointed out, Millard could be "inflexible," "uncommunicative," and "unwilling to change his vision when it didn't fit the reality of the marketplace." Ultimately, it was these shortcomings that brought an end to Millard's reign at ComputerLand.

A college dropout with no formal scientific training, Millard began working with computers in 1958 when his employer, Pacific Finance, purchased an early UNIVAC machine. His extensive computer skills earned him several promotions, but when further advancement was blocked by his lack of formal education he left the company to become director of data processing for Alameda County, California.

Millard earned an industrywide reputation for his brilliant computerization of government services. This led to a position as a state and municipal account specialist with IBM in 1961. Four years later, Millard left the giant computer company and became chief data processing engineer for San Francisco County, where he succeeded in repeating his earlier achievement of streamlining government operations.

Looking back on his career at the end of the 1960s, Millard could have taken justifiable pride in his accomplishments as a data processing specialist. Born 37 years earlier in a poor section of Oakland, he toiled at a number of menial jobs, including truck driver, gravel digger, and assembly line worker, before finding his niche as a computer professional.

But despite the generous salary and security afforded by his government job, Bill Millard was not satisfied working for someone else. As a youngster, he resented the fact that his father had chosen the safety of a dead-end clerical job with the Southern

Pacific Railroad over a riskier, but potentially more rewarding, career. The oldest of six children, Millard vowed early in life to succeed in a business of his own.

In 1969, he finally took a step toward fulfilling this dream by starting a software company, Systems Dynamics. The genius that Millard had displayed as a government employee would serve him well as an entrepreneur. Now that he was on his own, however, his fortunes would also be influenced by another personality factor—one that had been held in check when he had worked for others—his strong will. Millard's sharp single-mindedness was like a tool that cut both ways: it gave him the tenacity needed to overcome obstacles that would foil most entrepreneurs, but it also made him less able to adapt to changing situations.

This was apparent in the way Millard managed Systems Dynamics. Departing from conventional wisdom, which dictated that a new computer company should try to establish itself by filling an overlooked, specialized, market niche, Millard plunged his tiny software firm into direct competition with IBM. Not surprisingly, he failed to make any headway against the industry giant.

By 1972, Systems Dynamics was out of business, and the 40-year-old Millard was looking for a new way to support his wife and three daughters. Capitalizing on the reputation he had gained from his work with Alameda and San Francisco counties, he established IMS Associates, a data processing consulting firm.

In 1973, Millard landed a contract to set up a computer system for the New Mexico car dealerships owned by a young man named Philip Loring Reed III. Having underbid the contract initially, Millard was looking for a way to cut costs on the dealership's computer system when he learned of the new 8080 microprocessor developed by Intel. Using the relatively inexpensive Intel microprocessor and components from other manufacturers, Millard built his own low-cost microcomputer.

Millard called his microcomputer the IMSAI 8080. In the mid-1970s he formed the IMSAI Manufacturing Corporation and began marketing the computer in kit form, placing classified advertisements in *Popular Mechanics* and hobbyist magazines. At the time, only a few small companies, notably MITS and Processor Technology, were making computer kits. The IMSAI and other early microcomputers were sold mainly to hobbyists and engineers and marketed through the mail or by small specialty shops. Apple Computer and the personal computer boom were still two or three years down the road.

Although IMSAI's early sales were encouraging, the undercapitalized firm quickly ran out of cash. Millard could have raised capital through a public stock offering or by taking in investor-partners, but the stubbornly independent entrepreneur would tolerate no interference from outsiders.

Instead, in a move that would later come back to haunt him, Millard raised money by securing a $250,000 loan in early 1976 from Marriner & Co., a venture capital firm headed by the father of auto dealer Philip Loring Reed. Shortly after receiving the loan, Millard began to turn his attention away from IMSAI to a new business, and a nervous Marriner sought to protect itself by pressuring him to sign an agreement that gave it the right to convert its IOU into a 20 percent share of Millard's holding company, IMS Associates, and any other ventures he might start.

The new business that was occupying most of the 44-year-old entrepreneur's time was a computer store called Computer Shack that had opened on $10,000 capital. (The store's name was later changed to ComputerLand when Tandy Corporation, the owner of Radio Shack, threatened legal action.) Millard was inspired to start a computer store after his experience with the IMSAI 8080 convinced him that the small, casually run, independent shops that sold computer kits were ill-prepared to handle the growing demand for microcomputers on the part of small business owners and professionals.

"Anybody in the industry had the opportunity to observe this phenomenon," Millard once remarked.[2] And, indeed, a few other entrepreneurs did recognize the need for professionally run computer stores. But unlike ComputerLand, which carried products from a wide variety of manufacturers, most other stores confined their selections to specific brands of computers and thus had limited appeal for potential customers.

Convinced that the way to dominate the growing personal computer industry was to open a large number of stores early, Millard and his chief assistant, Edward Faber, embarked on a frenetic expansion program. The company had 24 stores doing $1.5 million in sales by the end of 1977, its first full year in business.

These numbers grew to 147 stores and $75 million in 1980, and over 580 stores and $963.4 million in 1983.

ComputerLand's great size served to compound its advantages over competing retailers. The chain was able to buy computers and peripheral gear in large quantities and earn generous discounts that it passed on to the consumer. Because of its marketing clout, ComputerLand was also able to obtain dealerships for the most desirable personal computer brands, a luxury not available to its smaller competitors. When IBM introduced its personal computer in August 1981, for example, only three retail chains were authorized to sell it—the company-owned IBM Product Centers, Sears Business Systems Centers, and Computer-Land.

William Millard accomplished this blitzkrieg expansion through franchising. With the exception of his pilot store, all ComputerLand outlets were franchised locations. Millard sold merchandise at cost to his franchisees, making his profits through franchise fees ($17,500 in 1977 and $75,000 in the early 1980s) and royalties (eight percent of sales plus an additional one percent for corporate advertising).

These high royalties eventually became a bone of contention with many ComputerLand franchisees, who argued that the company was not delivering enough merchandising and support services to justify its prices. "They provide four percent worth of services, but you pay for eight percent," a California franchisee complained to *Business Week* in 1985.[3]

Other franchisees argued that Millard had not kept pace with changes in the market. The price advantage that ComputerLand once enjoyed over its competitors had been all but wiped out in the mid-1980s by the dramatic overall decline in personal computer prices and the increased buying power of other chains. The company had also failed to develop an effective outside selling strategy for reaching large corporate accounts, which, by the mid-1980s, had become the fastest growing segment of the personal computer market.

Millard further alienated franchisees and executives at ComputerLand's central office when he named his 26-year-old daughter, Barbara Millard, president and chief operating officer of the company in November 1984. Like her father, Barbara Millard is a determined, highly energized person who exudes confidence. "I know I can do the job, and I'm ready," she declared soon after her appointment.[4] "She's just flat out bright, and her results are sufficiently outrageous to warrant her getting the job," added her father. Others, inside and outside Computerland, disagreed, questioning the wisdom of placing someone in her twenties with only a few months of college and limited business experience at the helm of a $1.5 billion company.

But William Millard's problems with disgruntled franchisees and associates were minor next to those that resulted from his legal battle with a former ComputerLand employee named John Martin-Musumeci. A one-time used car salesman, Martin-Musumeci was hired by ComputerLand as a franchise consultant in 1976. One year later, he was fired from the company. Unfortunately for Millard, this was not the last he was to hear from the short, animated consultant.

As part of his contract with ComputerLand, Martin-Musumeci received a 1.05% interest in the privately held company. In December 1980, he sold this interest to Bruno Andrighetto, a wealthy San Francisco produce dealer and stock market investor. Martin-Musumeci told Andrighetto about the outstanding Marriner IOU that was convertible to a 20 percent share of Millard's total business holdings, including ComputerLand. (By this time, the IMSAI Manufacturing Corporation had, as the venture capital firm had feared, gone bankrupt, taking most of its creditors down with it.)

Martin-Musumeci and Andrighetto formed a company called Micro-Vest, which purchased the Millard IOU from Marriner for $300,000 plus an agreement to pay another $100,000 should it ever convert the note into stock. In March 1981, two months before the IOU was to expire, Micro-Vest notified Millard (who had been dutifully paying interest on the note) of its intent to convert the note into a 20 percent share of ComputerLand stock.

William Millard refused to comply, arguing that the IOU was not transferable from Marriner and that a 20 percent share of IMS did not constitute an interest in ComputerLand. The case was dragged through the courts for four years before finally being decided in favor of Micro-Vest. Millard spent a reported $3 million during his losing court battle. Micro-Vest financed its legal expenses by selling shares in the IOU to outside investors, in-cluding former Bendix head William Agee and his wife, Mary Cunningham.

In addition to forcing Millard to turn over a 20 percent share of ComputerLand, the court ordered him to relinquish an equal amount of all other IMS holdings, including three corporate jets, a northern California vineyard, an Oregon ranch, and his own hillside home in the Piedmont section of Oakland.

Even more distressing to Millard, however, was the more than $141 million in damages and fees assessed against him. Under California law, Millard would have to post twice this amount ($283 million) as bond before he could appeal the court ruling. As wealthy as he was, Millard could not raise this much money without making a public offering of ComputerLand stock—something the intensely private entrepreneur was loathe to do.

Confronted with this no-win situation, William Millard stepped down as ComputerLand CEO in 1986 (his daughter, Bar-bara, also resigned as president) and began the painful process of extricating himself from his own company.

Lowell W. Paxson (1934-   )
Roy M. Speer (1932-   )

HOME SHOPPING NETWORK, INC.

"We knew we were on a rocket."

"It was absolute chaos. Traders were packed together scream-ing their bids and offers all day."

That was how Porter Morgan, vice-president of the American Stock Exchange, described the events of May 13, 1986, the day that Home Shopping Network (HSN) made its first public stock offering. It was one of the most explosive happenings in the his-tory of Wall Street. The Clearwater, Florida, firm's 2.3 million share offering opened the day at 18; by the time the closing bell rang that afternoon the stock was selling for 42-5/8, a 137 percent gain.

HSN stock continued its incredible odyssey in the days and weeks that followed. It soared past 60 by May 20 and reached 100 by mid-June, when the company announced a two-for-one split. Only Genentech, Inc., which jumped from 35 to 87 a share on its first day of trading, received a more enthusiastic reception on Wall Street in the 1980s.

Investors were drawn to HSN by the opportunity to get in on the ground floor of a promising new industry: direct selling on cable television. Described by *The New York Times* as the company that "brings mall shopping home,"[1] HSN differs from other TV

89

networks in that instead of selling commercial time to sponsors, it sells merchandise directly to viewers.

HSN's business works this way: The company's buyers scour American and overseas markets for closeouts, overruns, and other "deals" on everything from cameras, stereos, and appliances to apparel, bibles, and cubic zirconium jewelry. HSN shows this merchandise on its live, 24-hour-a-day, seven-day-a-week cable network, giving viewers a toll-free number they can call to place orders. Cable TV stations that carry HSN's "video shopping mall" receive a five percent commission on all sales made to viewers in their market.

Founded in 1982 by partners Lowell "Bud" Paxson, 48, and Roy M. Speer, 50, HSN is carried by over 325 stations in the U.S., Canada, Puerto Rico, and the Caribbean. The company's net earnings for the fiscal year ending August 31, 1986, were $17,046,000 on net sales of over $160 million.

Other companies had tried cable TV selling before HSN, but with the exception of a few firms that limited themselves to local markets, all of them went out of business. By becoming the first to succeed at selling products directly to viewers on a national network, HSN has pioneered an industry that many analysts predict will grow well past $1 billion by 1990.

There are many reasons why Paxson and Speer were able to succeed in a business that had baffled other cable marketing entrepreneurs. Unlike their predecessors, the HSN founders made it simple to order merchandise, requiring neither preenrollment in a club nor installation of computer hardware in the viewer's home. To order, the viewer simply calls the toll-free number shown on the TV screen and either gives the operator a major credit card number or sends a check to HSN.

Early cable marketers believed that consumers would gladly pay full retail prices for the convenience of shopping at home. But TV viewers, conditioned to commercials that offered discounts and rebates on every conceivable product, quickly rejected this approach. HSN, on the other hand, wooed these viewers by claiming to sell merchandise at discounts of up to 70 percent.

The most important innovation that Paxson and Speer brought to cable selling, however, involved neither simplified ordering nor discount prices, but showmanship. HSN was the first company to treat its direct marketing service as a program rather than an uninterrupted series of TV commercials. This allowed the company to compete with game shows, soap operas, and movies for viewer attention as "entertainment."

The HSN format is a glitzy hybridization of radio call-in program, "Wheel of Fortune," and TV evangelism. HSN broadcasts live and around-the-clock from a Florida studio that resembles a major network newsroom on election night. Instead of tracking results from the polls, however, the people in the studio are toll-free telephone operators, busily taking orders from viewer-shoppers.

On center stage, a "host" is extolling the value of a particular item, "normally $29.95, but we're not going to do it for $19, $15, or $12, but only $9.95." The viewer can take advantage of this bargain only during the time that the item is on the TV screen, which is never more than 10 minutes. HSN displays only one product at a time; once a product is taken off the air it cannot be purchased again—at least not until the next time it appears on the screen.

This creates the kind of excitement that keeps viewers watching; so, too, do the ringing cowbells and tooting bicycle horns that greet the on-the-air arrival of each new product, the clock that counts down the product's remaining time on stage, and the on-screen running tabulation of the product's sales figures.

First-time HSN callers receive five dollars off their purchase and are automatically enrolled in the Home Shopping Club, "the only club that pays you to join." HSN promotes a sense of belonging among club members by sending them birthday and anniversary cards containing "Spendable Kash" coupons.

This personal touch is reinforced by HSN hosts, a group of peppy, sparkling-faced young people with names like Budget Bob Circosta and Bubblin' Bobbi Ray. Hosts will often put a viewer-caller on the air live to chitchat about hometowns, families, and, of course, the fantastic bargain that the caller just received on a string of man-made pearls or a genuine leather briefcase.

Most of the more than one million Home Shopping Club members identify strongly with a particular host. Some will order merchandise only when a favorite personality is on the air. Budget Bob, the most popular host, receives an average of two thousand fan letters a week—some of them containing marriage proposals—from HSN viewers, about 80 percent of whom are women.

"I don't think you know the name of your clerk at K mart or Zayre, but you're going to know the name of our host," Bud Paxson once said.[2]

Much of the show business excitement that surrounds HSN is a direct outgrowth of Paxson's 30-year career in radio, as a talk show host and station owner. Born and raised in Rochester, New York, the HSN co-founder is a six-foot-six-inch, rail-thin man with an engaging manner and a salesman's enthusiasm. In the mid-1970s, Paxson owned WWQT, an AM station in Clearwater, Florida, that was rapidly losing listeners to its FM competitors. He switched to an all-talk format in an effort to regain market share, but still had a hard time lining up sponsors.

After returning to his office from a particularly discouraging sales call one day in 1977, Paxson was struck by a notion: "If we can't sell advertising, maybe we can sell product." Making the rounds of local merchants, he obtained a supply of distressed and overstocked merchandise. One week later, he went on the air with "Suncoast Bargaineers," a program that marketed discount merchandise directly to listeners. The show was an immediate success, and Paxson soon began devoting an increasing percentage of WWQT's airtime to direct selling.

When Clearwater was wired for cable TV in the early 1980s, the Florida entrepreneur decided to take his direct-selling concept to video. Paxson had the media experience and the natural salesmanship skills needed to make an in-home marketing service work on a local cable system. But before he could turn this idea into a large and successful company, he needed two additional things: a lot of capital, and some expertise in managing the mountain of paperwork that was sure to be created by a successful direct-selling cable channel.

He found both in Roy Speer.

Burly and low-keyed, Speer provides a sharp contrast to his HSN co-founder. A former assistant Florida attorney general, Speer had enjoyed considerable success in real estate, oil drilling, farming, and utilities. His career in government and business involved the managing of large organizations that relied heavily on computers to process volumes of paperwork. His was the perfect complement to Paxson's media background.

12. Paxson and Speer's studio in Clearwater, Florida—stage for the first successful national shop-at-home TV company, which reaped $160 million in sales in its fourth year.

In 1982, the partners launched their direct-selling venture on the Vision Cable System in Clearwater. Initially, the Home Shopping Channel, as it was then called, reached fewer than 200,000 cable subscribers in two Florida counties. Net sales the first year were only $898,000, but they increased to over $10 million in 1984, and Paxson and Speer considered expanding into Fort Lauderdale.

This plan was dropped in 1985, when the partners decided instead to take their home shopping service national. In July of that year, HSN became the first company to offer a nationwide direct-marketing service on television. It also became the first TV network to broadcast live, 24 hours a day, seven days a week.

The new shopping network was quickly embraced by viewers across the country. HSN earned $6.8 million on sales of $63.8 million in its first six months as a national network. During the same period, the number of people employed at the network's Florida headquarters tripled to a thousand. (By the end of 1986, the number of HSN employees increased to 2300.)

In March 1986, Paxson and Speer followed up their initial

success by launching a second shopping network, "HSN 2: Innovations in Modern Living." The new network features more upscale, name-brand merchandise (Gucci, Minolta, Pierre Cardin, and Yamaha) than the original network, "HSN 1: America's Biggest Bargain."

By mid-1986, HSN 1 and HSN 2 were reaching approximately 8.5 million homes. This number increased dramatically in the second half of the year, when the company began buying non-cable (UHF) TV stations in New York, Los Angeles, Boston, Baltimore, and other major markets. "We hope to become the fifth major TV network, right behind NBC, CBS, ABC, and Murdoch's new network," said Roy Speer when HSN announced its acquisition plans in August.

Psychologists and social scientists have yet to offer an explanation for HSN's incredible success. Many, undoubtedly, will question the implications of a network that beams a seductive mix of bargains and sales hype into American living rooms. Some of the more strident critics will accuse HSN of using its flashy stage props and exuberant sales hosts to manipulate viewers, many of them lonely, homebound people, into buying things that they neither want nor need.

Bud Paxson does not dispute the fact that HSN relies on impulse shopping. "People don't get up in the morning and say, 'I want to buy a hammer—I'd better watch TV,'" he explained.[3] "There's no way we fill a pre-existing need. What happens is, you watch, we create a need and then hopefully we fill it."

But to Paxson and HSN's large number of loyal viewers, the shopping network is much more than a purveyor of impulse merchandise. They see HSN as filling a need for an exciting and socially rewarding shopping experience that is as old as the market square and as modern as the regional mall.

"Years ago we all went into town, then to Main Street. Then we set up the mall," said Paxson.[4] Shopping's a reward for our good work, our good effort, the 40 hours you spent working during the week to buy yourself a little something. This allows us all to do that."

The rapid rise of HSN has propelled its founders into the ranks of the super-rich. In late 1986, Paxson's 45 percent share of HSN was worth $375 million, while Speer's 26 percent interest in the firm was valued at $220 million.[5]

Although both men were always confident that HSN would be an outstanding success, they were surprised by the company's phenomenal start. "We knew we were on a rocket," said Bud Paxson. "We just didn't know how high we'd go."[6]

Unfortunately for Paxson and Speer, the HSN "rocket" began a harrowing descent in the winter of 1987. The company's stock, which had been selling for $47 a share on January 21, dropped to 28\frac{1}{2}$ by February 18. The "paper worth" of HSN's founders declined proportionately; the value of Paxson's holdings went from $1.03 billion to $735 million and Speer's from $1.65 billion to $1.16 billion.[7]

HSN's decline on Wall Street coincided with announcements by two of the nation's retailing giants, Sears and J. C. Penney, that they planned to launch their own direct-selling cable TV programs. Like other pioneering entrepreneurs who had prospered by dominating a new market, Lowell Paxson and Roy Speer had to retrench and face the unpleasant reality that success breeds competition, but big success breeds big competition.

Ralph E. Schneider *(1909–1964)*

DINERS CLUB

"I had a good idea and worked hard, but I was very lucky, too."

Even now, almost 40 years after Ralph Schneider, the late Diners Club co-founder, introduced the first general-purpose credit card, his son Bob still hears the occasional groans of unlucky investors who missed their golden opportunity.

"I'll run into someone on the street, and they'll say, 'You know, your father came to me looking for money when he started, but I turned him down,' " remarked the New York stockbroker. "They feel bad when they think of what they could have made by getting in on the ground floor of Diners Club. But back then, they all thought that my father's idea for a credit card was crazy."

Although the ultimate success of the credit card would show them to be very wrong, these would-be investors had every reason to be skeptical in 1949, when they were approached by the 40-year-old Schneider and his partner, Frank X. McNamara, 33. The Diners Club card that the two men planned to introduce was unlike anything the world had ever seen.

There were, to be sure, other credit cards before Diners Club. Oil companies had pioneered the credit card concept back in the 1920s with gasoline charge cards. They were soon followed by department stores, airlines, hotels, and other businesses that issued cards to their regular customers. But these early credit cards were really no more than merchandising tools, offered as a customer convenience and used only to purchase the goods or services sold by the issuing company.

The Diners Club card created by Schneider and McNamara operated under a completely different concept. Unlike its predecessors, Diners Club was a "freestanding" card, independent of any outside company. Sold to customers on its own merits rather than as part of a specific firm's marketing plan, the card could be used at a variety of different businesses, giving it at least some of the flexibility of cash.

Exactly how Schneider and McNamara hit upon the idea for their unique all-purpose credit card is uncertain. According to one often-quoted tale, Diners Club grew out of an embarrassing experience McNamara had at an expensive restaurant, when he found himself short of cash after being presented with his bill.

This story, though, is based more on the imagination of a press agent than on fact. "It's a nice anecdote," said Bob Schneider. "McNamara is supposed to have told my father about this experience one day when they were having lunch, and my father was supposed to have said, 'Gee, that wouldn't have happened if you had a credit card'—and bingo, they created Diners Club."

In reality, the Diners Club idea evolved out of many conversations between Schneider and McNamara. Both men were active in New York business circles; Schneider was an attorney, and McNamara was his client and good friend. Both realized from personal experience that the trend toward expense account dining was creating a need for an all-purpose restaurant credit card.

But neither partner envisioned Diners Club becoming a national corporation. "I don't think they ever imagined it going beyond the city when they started," Bob Schneider told the authors of this book.

Schneider and McNamara may have viewed Diners Club as a small, specialized service, but a profound upheaval in the American business landscape was about to place their little company on top of a corporate mountain.

Companies were rapidly becoming more national in scope following World War II, as mergers and acquisitions created giant conglomerates with offices scattered across the country; and the relatively new practice of franchising led to the development of coast-to-coast chains of restaurants, hotels, and retail stores. The growing dominance of national companies, together with advances in air and highway transportation (the interstate system was then being developed), created a sharp increase in business travel. This, in turn, led to more expense account spending.

A freestanding credit card like Diners Club provided the business traveler with a convenient way to pay for and record meals, hotel bills, and other expense account items. Business travelers became especially interested in the record-keeping value of credit cards in 1958, when the Internal Revenue Service began to require the itemization of all expense account deductions.

Propelled by these market forces, Diners Club expanded with the speed of a forest fire. Only one year after its inception, the company had signed up 35,000 cardholders in more than a half-dozen cities across the country. These Diners Club members could use their cards at 275 restaurants and nightclubs—including New York's Copacabana, Los Angeles' Ciro's, and Chicago's Blackhawk—as well as at hotels, florist shops, gourmet shops, and automobile rental agencies.

In 1952, Diners Club expanded its service into Europe. By the time the company had celebrated its eighth anniversary, five years later, its card was honored at some 17,000 establishments in 76 nations, its membership roster exceeded 700,000, and total annual billings were $140 million.

But these figures would have seemed unbelievable to any potential investor back when Diners Club was getting started. Schneider and McNamara were unable to interest a single outsider in their new venture and were forced to raise $55,000 in start-up capital themselves—Schneider borrowing about $8000 from his mother, Minnie.

In February 1950, the two men started Diners Club in a three-room suite on the 24th floor of the Empire State Building. (As their business later grew, Schneider and McNamara moved into larger and loftier quarters in the famous skyscraper, relocating twice within a year of Diners Club's founding, first to offices on the 32nd floor and then to a spacious suite on the 77th floor.)

The partners' first order of business was to sell restaurants on the Diners Club idea. "We thought the man on the street would go for it, but we weren't sure about the restaurants," Ralph Schneider later recalled.[1]

The reluctance of restaurant owners to join Diners Club was understandable. Schneider and McNamara planned to take a seven percent fee out of all meals charged on their cards (excluding tips) to cover the cost of billing cardholders and absorbing bad debts. Persuading restaurant owners to part with seven percent of their tabs was no easy task. But Schneider and Mc-

Namara convinced them that this fee would be more than offset by the added traffic that Diners Club would bring to their establishments. Furthermore, as many restaurateurs had already discovered with their own in-house credit programs, customers tended to order more lavishly when they could charge a meal on the cuff.

Within a month, Schneider and McNamara had signed up fourteen Manhattan restaurants. Their next step was to build a roster of Diners Club members. Working from a mailing list of 5000 sales executives (purchased for $75), they enrolled 75 charter members in the club. Diners Club gained momentum throughout the remainder of the year, expanding at a rate of 800 new members a week.

But then Schneider and McNamara noticed a disturbing pattern: despite its rapid expansion, the company was consistently losing money. "The restaurants were happy, and the cardholders were happy," Schneider once commented.[2] "The only ones who weren't happy were us, because the operating cost far exceeded our commission and we weren't making any money."

Schneider and McNamara solved this problem late in their first year by implementing a three-dollar annual membership fee (soon upped to five dollars). Not only did the membership fee bring in added income every year, it also pressured members who rarely used their Diners Club cards to drop out, reducing the expense of processing inactive accounts. In its second year of operation, Diners Club earned an after-tax profit of $61,222 on a volume of $6.2 million. The company's profits continued to climb throughout the 1950s, reaching close to $2 million by the end of the decade.

Inspired by the success of Diners Club, other companies rushed into the credit card market. *Esquire,* Duncan Hines, Universal Air Travel Plan, and *Gourmet* magazine all introduced their own cards in the early 1950s, as did major banks in many cities. But these "bank cards," the forerunners of the modern VISA and Mastercard, were used primarily at local stores rather than restaurants and hotels, and were not in direct competition with Diners Club.

Many of Schneider and McNamara's early restaurant card competitors quickly folded for lack of capital or management skills. The more formidable ones were acquired by Diners Club, including Dine 'n Sign, a Los Angeles–based firm founded by

Alfred S. Bloomingdale, the playboy scion of the department store family.

Bloomingdale became Schneider's sole partner in Diners Club in 1952, after Frank McNamara left the company to start a mail order business. (McNamara died of a heart attack five years later at the age of 40.) According to Bob Schneider, the relationship between his father and Alfred Bloomingdale was not a particularly close one. "The two of them were as different as night and day. My father was very quiet and conservative, and Bloomingdale was a flashy, fast-talking type."

Nevertheless, Diners Club continued to prosper with Schneider as its chief executive officer and Bloomingdale as its president. When the two men made the first public offering of Diners Club stock in 1955, selling 100,000 of their combined 400,000 shares, each received $350,000. By 1959, Schneider's holdings in the company were worth over $12 million.

The success of Diners Club made Ralph Schneider something of a celebrity in business circles. He was featured on the cover of *Business Week* and was the subject of lengthy articles in other magazines. He also appeared in advertisements, endorsing business products like Mosler safes.

A neatly manicured man of medium height and weight, Schneider led a life typical of an urbane Manhattan millionaire of the 1950s. He lived in an elegant eight-room apartment in the Hotel Pierre overlooking Central Park, wintered in a Caribbean mountaintop mansion, and was chauffeured in a shiny black Cadillac limousine.

"Make no mistake about it, my father enjoyed all the trappings of wealth," said Bob Schneider. "He enjoyed dining at New York's best restaurants, where everybody knew him, and people were always coming up to him to ask for his opinion about this or that business deal. At the same time, though, he remained a very modest man. People would always say, 'Mr. Schneider, what do you attribute your great success to?' And he'd tell them, 'I got lucky. I had a good idea and worked hard, but I was very lucky too.'"

Ralph Schneider was undoubtedly a lucky man; lucky that no one was willing to invest in Diners Club in its first year, when a large share of the company could have been had for a fraction of what it would ultimately be worth, and lucky that his idea for a small, local credit card venture put him at the forefront of a major new trend. But Schneider was not a gambler who happened to draw four aces. A graduate of the University of Pennsylvania and Harvard Law School, the Bronx-born attorney was a nimble-minded man whose ability to react quickly to changing market conditions served him well in business. As head of Diners Club, he successfully built on the company's early lead in the credit card market by adopting a policy of acquiring smaller competitors. He facilitated further expansion and protected his flank against new competition by aggressively opening branch offices in other cities and franchising Diners Club operations in Europe.

Schneider's biggest challenge as an executive occurred when a powerful new competitor, traveler's check giant American Express, entered the credit card market in 1958, followed one year later by the Hilton Corporation's well-financed Carte Blanche. Faced with serious competition for the first time, Diners Club responded by lowering its seven percent commission for high-volume accounts and embarking on an aggressive membership campaign. The company also made a tangible improvement in its product in 1961, when it replaced the paper credit cards it had been using with plastic cards.

As a further competitive gambit, Schneider planned to invade American Express' traveler's check market by introducing Diners Club traveler's checks. This plan was dropped, however, because of his failing health. "My father had a very bad heart," said Bob Schneider. "He had a serious heart attack right around the time he started Diners Club, and he had several minor ones in the years that followed.

"The doctors told him to slow down, but he took the attitude, 'I'd rather live life to the fullest, even it means losing a few years.' He was very fatalistic about his heart condition. He always figured that when his time was up he would go, but until then. . . . "

Ralph Schneider was stricken with a fatal heart attack on Monday evening, November 2, 1964, at the Hotel Pierre. He was 55 years old. A few months later, Diners Club completed its most successful fiscal year, earning $2.7 million in after-tax profits. Although American Express would more than double the billings of Diners Club by the start of the next decade, Ralph Schneider had successfully fought off its challenge in the last years of his life.

13. William C. Norris (center) at the New York Stock Exchange on March 6, 1963, when Control Data Corp. was first listed on the Big Board. The price of CDC stock would fluctuate wildly over the next two decades, reflecting the erratic performance of the computer company.

IV

Plugging
a Gap

David A. Norman *(1935–   )*

BUSINESSLAND, INC.

"There was an opportunity to build a very large company very quickly in a whole new industry."

In 1985, David Norman had the honor of being chosen by *Computer Retail News* as number one on the magazine's list of the top twenty-five executives in the computer retailing industry for the year. A photo of the youthful-looking Businessland founder is shown on the magazine's cover at the top of a "stairway," above such rivals as William Millard of ComputerLand, who finished number two.[1]

The accompanying feature story calls 1985 a "year of vindication" for Norman, who had started Businessland with $3.5 million capital three years earlier. It marked the first time the San Jose, California, chain turned a profit, after losing $1.2 million and $4.7 million respectively in fiscal 1983 and 1984. Although the take-home was slim—$239,000 on sales of $267 million—it was enough to silence Norman's critics in the industry and on Wall Street who had doubted that his idea for a store that sold microcomputers to business users only would ever get off the ground.

The skeptics had found two major flaws in Businessland's marketing plan. First, they asked, why would a company buy a computer through a middleman—in this case, a Businessland store—when the same piece of equipment could be purchased more cheaply direct from the manufacturer?

Second, Norman's strategy for reaching his intended market

105

of business customers was neither fish nor fowl. What the California entrepreneur was proposing was not quite a walk-in retail store and not quite a direct-selling network, but a costly hybridization of the two. On one hand, his plan called for a chain of Businessland centers in expensive strip locations, which would draw the many small-business owners who were computerizing their offices and warehouses but whose several-thousand-dollar average purchase wouldn't be enough to justify a personal sales call. At the same time, Norman planned to send out a technically trained direct-sales force to call on larger corporations with more complex equipment needs, thereby competing against IBM and other manufacturers who were actively pursuing this segment of the market.

Having it both ways would be a costly proposition for Norman. His company would have to make enough margin on its products to support this dual overhead burden. And it would have to do so at a time, as critics pointed out, when other retailers were scrambling to undersell each other and the glutted microcomputer market was becoming more price-sensitive every day.

That was why the watershed year of 1985 was, indeed, a vindication for the 50-year-old Norman. Not only did Businessland operate in the black for the first time, right on schedule with its founder's prediction, but it did so when most other computer retailers were reporting a decline in profits and sales due to price cutting and a slowdown in consumer demand.

In going against the industry downturn, Norman was held up as a shining example by the trade and business press. Two months before the *Computer Retail News* feature appeared, *Business Week* ran a story entitled, "How To Sell Computers Today—And How Not To," contrasting the marketing strategies of the Businessland head with those of ComputerLand rival Millard.[2]

William Millard had built ComputerLand into the nation's largest computer retail chain in the 1970s by buying computers at volume discounts and selling them to home users through franchised outlets. But, as *Business Week* pointed out, his formula was no longer working. The mid-1980s had brought about increased competition from independent stores, which, because they did not have to pay franchise royalties, could undercut ComputerLand's prices. Norman, on the other hand, was praised

for "targeting business customers exclusively" and thereby avoid-
ing "the more price-sensitive home and education markets." Furthermore, since commercial customers tended to make bigger
purchases, Businessland's average system sale was $6000 versus
ComputerLand's $2000.

When presented with such frequently drawn comparisons,
however, David Norman insists that although the two chains may
have similar-sounding names, his company is not a Burger King
to ComputerLand's McDonald's.

"We're aiming at entirely different markets," said the trim,
vigorous California executive. "From the beginning, our concept
was to focus on the business market. We were never interested
in the home computer market. Although we may look like a retailer, we're not. A business can't do everything. It needs to focus
on a few specific things and do them well."

Norman's two decades of experience with Silicon Valley companies got him focused on the idea of establishing a chain of
stores that sold computers exclusively to businesses. A former
Lockheed engineer who later started two high-tech consulting
firms of his own, he had dealt with enough corporate executives
to see that most companies needed guidance in sorting their way
through the increasingly complex maze of business automation
equipment.

Seated at his desk at his company's no-frills San Jose headquarters, Norman described how the Businessland concept took
shape. "I saw there was a need for a professional service that
would advise businesses in choosing the right computer system
for their needs, and would also train the customer how to use
the system to its full potential.

"The advantage we would offer over a manufacturer is that
we would give the customer equipment options from many different sources. No one manufacturer has all the hardware and
software solutions. One customer might be best served by an IBM
computer, someone else's printer, and a couple of other manufacturers' software. We would put the components together into
an integrated system, test it, and train the customer to operate
it."

Competition from manufacturers did not worry Norman for
another reason: he felt it would actually decrease in the future
as high-tech products came down in price. "No manufacturer

would be able to afford to maintain its own direct sales force calling on customers when prices and profit margins got lower, as they inevitably would. But a company like ours could set up a high-quality distribution channel that would be cost-efficient, because we would be selling products from manufacturers all over the world, and we would be reaching all levels of the business market—from a small accounting office to a Fortune 500 company."

The Businessland plan was developed in 1982, at a time when Norman, then 47, was at a crossroads in his career. Four years earlier, he had sold his high-tech consulting firm, Dataquest, Inc., to the A. C. Nielsen Co. after the giant conglomerate "made an offer impossible to refuse." Norman had stayed on to run Dataquest and become a director at Nielsen, but grew increasingly restless once he realized there was nowhere else for him to advance to.

"I saw I wasn't going to get to run Nielsen," said Norman, a three-mile-a-day jogger, who skis and flies his own single-engine Piper Malibu. "I had all this high energy, so I started looking around."

Norman looked at "everything from leverage buyouts to other types of high-tech companies," but his mind kept going back to the idea of a store that sold computers to businesses. "I saw there was an opportunity to build a very large company very quickly in a whole new industry. It was an opportunity to set up a whole new distribution channel. Going out and developing a high-tech product might have been fine, but the key was, who was going to service the customer out there. That's where the real power is in the long term."

Although his idea would later come under fire from second-guessers, Norman had no trouble raising the capital needed to start Businessland. His standing was excellent with area venture capital firms like Oak Investment Partners and Bessemer Venture Partners, where he had co-invested some of the proceeds from the Dataquest sale in new high-tech start-ups. These connections, together with Norman's track record of starting successful companies—Dataquest and an earlier consulting firm called Creative Strategies—were enough to attract $3.5 million in the first of three preferred stock offerings.

Dataquest was responsible for bringing another asset to the

new Businessland company: a bearded Italian electronics expert named Enzo Torresi. As the president of an Olivetti subsidiary in Cupertino, California, Torresi had been a client of Data-quest's; he was chosen by Norman as number two man to "bring some credibility on the product side of the plan."

"Enzo's one of the most technically knowledgeable people in the microcomputer field, and I felt that with his expertise in the product end, and my ability as a manager, we'd make an unbeatable team," Norman said.

The first Businessland store was opened in November 1982 in San Jose. Four years—and two major acquisitions—later, the California company had a string of 150 locations in 50 markets from coast to coast, selling IBM, Compaq, Apple, Hewlett-Packard, Toshiba, and its own private-label products.

Unlike ComputerLand's franchised outlets, all Businessland units are company-owned, something Norman believes is essential for delivering a high level of customer service. "To do what we're doing, you've got to have complete control," he stated. The control extends to the physical environment of Businessland stores, whose 6000-square-foot, green-and-gold interiors have identical layouts: an open central area where computer systems

14. Lean and vigorous, former Navy fighter pilot David Norman looks a good deal younger than his 51 years. A tireless worker, Norman put in 90-hour weeks for two years after he founded Businessland in 1982. Once the retail computer chain was established, he "scaled down" to 60-hour weeks. (*Copyright Businessland, Inc. Photographer: Dana Gluckstein*)

are displayed in work station clusters, flanked by a "Service Center" and a "Learning Center." All products, down to accessories like printer ribbons and diskettes, occupy the exact same spot in each store. "If a customer from Chicago, say, takes a business trip to Dallas and stops in at a Businessland center to buy software, he'll know exactly where to find it," explained Norman.

The stores combined have a direct-selling staff of one thousand, which places Businessland in the top four computer marketing companies in the U.S. In 1985, the firm lavished $600 per month in training for each of its salespeople, prompting one computer trade publication to observe that the San Jose company "has driven for market position, sacrificing earnings in the quest."

But David Norman sees training as an investment in his company's long-term growth, explaining that the emphasis in the computer marketing industry is shifting to larger corporations that require more specialized selling. "What has surprised us most is the extent of the demand for our service among medium and large companies," said Norman with his slightly nasal intonation. "Initially, we thought we'd be serving mostly small-business customers. But our real strength has been with the corporate giants. We do business with 34 of the top Fortune 50."

Government has been another unexpectedly responsive client. In December 1985, the state of California awarded Businessland a contract to open a store in Sacramento exclusively for serving the automation needs of its agencies and departments. The company has also been called upon by the federal government to install a computer system at the White House.

Growth, in any and all directions, is welcomed by the company founder, who has set the goal of reaching the $1 billion milestone by 1990. "We need to be a billion-dollar player to be a factor in the market, so we'll continue to drive for that," he stated, following the announcement of Businessland's acquisition of the MBI Business Centers chain in April 1986. By the end of fiscal 1986, the company was halfway to its targeted billion-dollar mark.

At this stage, thinking in ten-figure terms seems quite natural for Norman, who regards his success at Businessland as the logical culmination of a career spent moving ahead "one step at a time."

"Success is the result of confidence. And confidence comes from being successful at the things you do," he explained. "You have to take it a step at a time, and as you succeed at each step, you become more self-confident. Then you can push yourself to take even bigger risks, and build even more confidence."

Norman regards his tour of duty as a Navy pilot in the late 1950s as one of the most influential experiences in his life. "I made several hundred landings on Navy aircraft carriers. And every week we were given tests in flight training; you either passed or went out and did something else."

Later, after earning a B.S. in mechanical engineering from the University of Minnesota, Norman took a job with Lockheed. There he worked on a nine-month design project with seventy-five other engineers and finished first in his class—another confidence-building experience.

"As a reward, Lockheed sent me for further study at Stanford. But once I got there and took some courses in management and other subjects, I saw I didn't want to spend the rest of my career in production engineering—it was too limited."

Norman stayed on a couple of years working at Stanford Research Institute, where he acquired a "broad background in management consulting." That led to the formation of Creative Strategies, Inc., with a partner in 1969. But two years later, tired of being "the number two guy," he left to start his own consulting firm, Dataquest, which he built into a $20 million company.

After the 1978 sale of Dataquest to Nielsen, Norman had the liquidity, reputation, and—most importantly—the vision and confidence to orchestrate his biggest venture to date, Businessland. "Each step prepared me for the next," he summed up. "Really, it was all very logical."

William C. Norris (1911–)

CONTROL DATA CORPORATION

"Address society's unmet needs as profitable business opportunities."

In a typical scenario, an entrepreneur with a lot of creative drive and a strong gambler's instinct hits upon a good idea and starts a company. Then, once the company has passed a certain point on its growth curve, the entrepreneur either changes his or her risk-taking ways or turns the company over (with varying degrees of reluctance) to more conservative professional managers.

William Norris, the crusty, tough-talking founder of Control Data Corporation (CDC), is the exception that proves this rule. For almost 30 years, Norris ran his multi-billion-dollar company like a small, backroom engineering shop. Exhibiting all of the impulsive enthusiasm of a start-up entrepreneur, he preferred gut feeling to market surveys and seat-of-the-pants judgments to committee reports. During his long and controversial career, he pushed CDC into an eclectic variety of products and services, from "supercomputers" and peripheral gear to an Hawaiian windmill farm and vocational training programs for prison inmates.

Many of Norris's corporate moves were absolutely brilliant; others were disastrous. Not surprisingly, CDC's fortunes rose and fell with the precipitousness of a riverboat gambler's during Norris's reign as president and CEO.

Founded in 1957 by Norris and a group of other computer

engineers, the company's net income zigzagged from $1.5 million in 1962 to minus-$1.9 million in 1966 to $51.7 million in 1969 to minus-$3.2 million in 1970 to $124 million in 1979 to minus-$567 million in 1985, Norris's last year in office. CDC's performance on the Big Board has been equally erratic; in one four-year period (1969–72), the company's stock went, without splitting, from 159¼ to 28¾, back up to 85 and down again to 42½.

Under Norris, CDC pioneered some of the computer industry's most significant new products such as the Model 6600, the first superpowerful computer intended for scientific applications. It also muddled through many costly dead-end projects such as PLATO, a computer-based education system that consumed hundreds of millions of dollars in R&D funds over a 20-year period before it turned its first small profit in 1983.

William Norris started his career in what is now called the computer industry during World War II, when he became a member of the Navy's crack code-breaking team, the Communications Supplementary Activity group, pronounced "Seesaw" and commonly referred to as "CSAW." As a member of CSAW, Norris worked with the electronic storage devices and tabulating machines that were the forerunners of modern computer equipment.

After the war, Norris and a group of other CSAW veterans formed, with the Navy's encouragement, a company called Engineering Research Associates (ERA) in Minneapolis to develop highly specialized electronic data processing equipment. Lacking capital, the young engineers sold a 50 percent share of their company to an investment banker named John Parker for $200,000. It was a decision that the fiercely independent Norris would later have cause to regret.

ERA did moderately well for a few years, selling customized electronic equipment to the Navy and a handful of defense contractors. But real growth could not be achieved unless the company created products with a more generalized commercial application. Developing and producing these products would require a large influx of working capital, which John Parker proposed to raise by merging ERA with a larger corporation. Norris and the other CSAW veterans were adamantly opposed to this idea, fearing that they would lose their creative freedom as research engineers once ERA was absorbed into a giant partner's corporate bureaucracy.

But, as ERA's major shareholder, Parker had no difficulty imposing his will on the company. In December 1951, he sold ERA to the business machine behemoth Remington Rand for close to two million dollars. (John Parker received half of this money for his 50 percent interest in ERA.) A quarter of a century later, the sale of ERA still rankled Bill Norris.

"It was one of the stupidest business decisions of all time," snapped the fiesty 75-year-old computer pioneer. "He got one million dollars from the sale, but had he waited just a few years his holdings in the company would have been worth a hundred million dollars."

Norris and virtually all of the ERA engineers remained with the company following the sale to Remington Rand. At the time, the New York business machine maker was the undisputed leader of the embryonic computer industry as a result of its acquisition of ERA and another firm, Philadelphia's Eckert-Mauchly, makers of the first commercial computer, the UNIVAC One.

Despite this early lead, Remington Rand's efforts in computers were marred by constant infighting and bureaucratic bungling. Many of the company's top managers had little or no appreciation of the new machine's importance. Others regarded the computer as a threat to their own special projects and prevented it from receiving the necessary R&D support. Hampered by this petty and inefficient bureaucracy, UNIVAC lost its dominant position to the aggressive and well-organized IBM company.

The problems at UNIVAC grew worse in 1956, when the parent company, then called Sperry Rand, hired a consultant who greatly curtailed the power of Norris and other "ERA people." In 1957, Norris led an exodus of former ERA engineers, including Willis Drake (see profile on page 136), to form a new computer company, Control Data Corp., in Minneapolis. "It got very frustrating sitting there watching a company squander a tremendous opportunity," said Norris. The Sperry Rand experience taught him a valuable lesson: "To really run a computer company successfully, you had to have top executives who understood computers." This was a point that Sperry Rand had obviously failed to grasp, and it was one that Norris intended to adhere to at Control Data.

Another lesson that the 45-year-old Norris and his associates had learned from experience was not to allow any single investor to have a controlling interest in the company. Not wanting to re-peat the situation where a John Parker could dictate policy to the rest of the company, the group decided to raise capital by selling shares in Control Data to a large number of independent inves-tors. In what was then a very unconventional move for a business with no assets, no facility, and no proven product, CDC made a public offering of 600,000 one-dollar shares. This was the first time that a start-up company attempted to raise seed money through a public stock sale.

The early experiment in venture capital financing was a re-sounding success. CDC more than doubled its initial subscrip-tion, selling 1.4 million shares.

Although he never owned a majority interest in the company, Norris was its undisputed leader from the start. "My plan is Con-trol Data's plan," he once said,[1] and in the late 1950s that plan could be summed up in one sentence: "Hit IBM where they are weakest."

Rather than try to compete against IBM with a medium-power business computer, as UNIVAC was doing with dismal results, Control Data entered the market with a bigger supercomputer for scientific applications. Norris and the other CDC engineers were well-versed in the subject of large-scale computers, having developed one of the earliest scientific machines, the ERA 1103, back in their days at ERA.

Control Data's first large-scale computer, the Model 1604, was introduced eight months after the company's founding. De-signed by former ERA engineer Seymour Cray, the 1604 distin-guished itself by using transistorized circuit cards instead of the slower vacuum tubes. The company sold its first $1.5 million computer to an old ERA customer, the U.S. Navy. Following the sale, orders poured in from government agencies, universities, and other large institutional users, allowing CDC to establish an important beachhead in the computer market.

By 1961, Control Data, which claimed a 1.6 percent share of the computer market, and IBM, with an 82 percent share, were the only companies making money in computers. The computer divisions of major corporations like Bendix, RCA, Honeywell, and Philco were all operating in the red, while one-time industry leader Sperry Rand was just about breaking even.

Then, in the mid-1960s, the CDC roller coaster took its first

15. Control Data officers Frank Mullaney and George Hanson look on as William Norris (left) shakes hands with a representative of North American Van Lines upon delivery of the first 1604 computer. In the early 1960s, CDC used the large-scale computer to carve out a niche against IBM, which was weakest in the upper end of the market.

dip. In 1964, the company introduced the Seymour Cray–designed Model 6600, a six-foot-tall, seven-ton honeycomb of 350,000 transistors capable of processing three million instructions per second. Although it was more powerful than anything on the market, the $5 million machine was plagued by technical difficulties in its early years. This problem was made worse by the tendency of overzealous CDC salespeople to make wildly exaggerated claims for the 6600's performance.

Norris's engineers were in the process of debugging the 6600 in 1966 when IBM introduced its own supercomputer, the 360–90. This new competition from the industry's dominant company sent CDC reeling. Earnings, which had been at 58 cents a share for the first half of 1965, fell to minus-5 cents for the corresponding period in 1966.

Rumors circulated on Wall Street that CDC was about to go out of business, but Bill Norris was not the kind of man to give up without a fight. A seasoned computer veteran, he knew that it was just a matter of time before the 6600's problems were solved. He knew, too, that IBM's new supermachine was bound to run into bugs of its own.

116

Valiantly, Norris pressed ahead with the development of the 6600. He also pressed ahead with a lawsuit against IBM, charging the company with unfair trade practices. Everything turned out as Bill Norris had hoped: the 6600 was debugged; his legal action ended in a generous out-of-court settlement; and, in March 1967, difficulties with the 360–90 led IBM to announce that it was no longer taking orders for the machine.

With his company's niche in large-scale computers firmly established, Norris began to diversify into computer timesharing (a service that sells computing time on a mainframe computer to small outside users), computer technician training, computer peripherals like disk drives and printers, and, in the noncomputer field, a financial services company called Commercial Credit.

By the end of the 1960s, CDC had seemingly solidified its position as the computer industry's number two profit leader, and Norris was talking confidently of becoming "the Ford of the computer industry" to IBM's General Motors.

It is interesting that William Norris once chose to compare CDC to Ford, because he shares much in common with the automobile company's legendary founder. Both men grew up on midwestern farms (Norris in Nebraska, Ford in Michigan); both were shy, strong-willed geniuses who became pioneers in the development of major industries; both ruled their companies with iron-clad authority for long periods; and both became very involved in what they perceived as important causes.

Just as Henry Ford had his isolationism (he was an outspoken critic of U.S. involvement in both world wars), William Norris has had his social activism. The CDC founder has often been quoted as saying that corporations should "address society's major unmet needs as profitable business opportunities." True to his word, he has built plants in ghettos, furnished schools and prisons with educational programs, provided data bank services to small businesses and farmers, experimented with farming in the Alaskan tundra, and, in the interest of promoting better international understanding, has scheduled a CDC board meeting behind the Iron Curtain. (The site of the 1977 meeting had to be switched hastily from Bucharest, Rumania, to Vienna, Austria, following an earthquake.)

No one would argue with Norris's goal of building a better

117

world, but many at CDC questioned whether his social programs had a place in a public corporation. "Bill doesn't just want to be in business, he wants to save the world too," one former CDC executive said in 1983.[2] "He doesn't run the corporation for profits and share holders," another executive commented two years later. "He runs it for Bill Norris."[3]

These former executives and others complained that by pouring money into social ventures that produced little or no profits, Norris was depriving the company of the research and development funds it needed to keep pace with its rapidly changing market. This became readily apparent in the late 1970s and early 1980s, when the company's new products were consistently late, overpriced, and out of touch with consumer demand. A case in point is CDC's problem-plagued 5¼-inch disk drive. Competing peripheral manufacturers introduced the small disk drives in 1977, and they quickly became the choice of personal computer makers. But CDC did not begin producing them until 1980. Then, in 1981, other manufacturers shifted production to offshore facilities, lowering the average price of a disk drive from $150 to $75. Again, CDC was slow to respond, not shifting its production until 1984, leaving itself with a large inventory of overpriced products.

With CDC's troubles continuing to mount, William Norris resigned as chairman and CEO on January 10, 1986. Like Henry Ford, he left behind a mixed legacy, his era one of forceful and innovative management marred by the occasional excesses that can occur when a creative entrepreneur goes too far without the advice of responsible corporate managers.

Sam A. Sarno *(1917–)*

SEVEN OAKS INTERNATIONAL

"The market was wide open—you could not help but make money."

Grocery coupons have been around since the turn of the century, but it wasn't until the 1960s, with its increased emphasis on consumerism, that they began to appear in significant numbers.

To an independent grocer like Sam Sarno of Memphis, Tennessee, the growth of coupons was a mixed blessing. He appreciated the additional store traffic that coupon promotions created, but the cost involved in sorting and processing redeemed coupons often eclipsed the small handling fee he received from the issuing company.

"The big grocery chains had their coupons processed for them by clearinghouses like A. C. Nielsen," said Sarno. "But the independent grocer didn't do enough volume for a company like Nielsen to bother with, so he was pretty much left to handle coupons on his own. This meant sorting them by manufacturer, counting them, doing the paperwork, and waiting for your money. It was time-consuming work, and the average grocer had much more important things to do with his time."

As coupons became more prevalent, an idea began to form in Sarno's mind: Why not start a clearinghouse that specialized in serving independent grocers? Under Sarno's plan, a grocer would send all of his redeemed coupons to the clearinghouse, which would count and sort them and mail the grocer a redemption check. Sarno would then forward the processed cou-

119

16. Memphis grocer Sam Sarno could not get big clearinghouses like A. C. Nielsen to process his manufacturers' coupons. This inspired Sarno to found Seven Oaks International, a clearinghouse specializing in small-volume accounts, in 1971.

pons to the issuing manufacturer for reimbursement. His clearinghouse would make its profit by keeping all, or part, of the eight-cents-per-coupon handling fee that the issuer normally paid to the grocer.

Raising $100,000, Sarno, his brother-in-law Joseph Radogna, and a group of Memphis investors turned this plan into a reality in 1971 when they formed Seven Oaks International. The 54-year-old grocer could not have picked a better time to enter the coupon redemption business. As the 1970s unfolded, the coupon trend that had been a distinct, but distant, rumble during the previous decade erupted with full volcanic force. Runaway inflation and an epidemic of shortages of everything from beef to coffee sent nervous shoppers looking for anything that could save them money at the supermarket. Coupons were a ready, albeit imperfect, solution.

A statistical look at the decade gives some idea of how the coupon industry exploded. Between 1970 and 1979, the total number of manufacturer's coupons distributed in the U.S. jumped from 16.4 billion to 81.2 billion. By the end of the decade, 76 percent of American households were clipping coupons at least occasionally, compared to 58 percent in 1971.[1]

Seven Oaks rode this trend to success. The volume of coupons processed by the clearinghouse leapt from 48 million in 1976 to 214 million in 1979 to over a billion in 1986.

"We went in at the right time and right place, and things just started growing for us," Sam Sarno acknowledged. "The market was wide open, and you could not help but make money in it."

Good timing undoubtably contributed to the early success of Seven Oaks, but Sam Sarno did not just open the door, turn on the lights and watch his business grow. Not only was Sarno astute enough to recognize the coupon trend in its earliest stages, he also had the managerial skills and experience needed to take advantage of his golden opportunity.

"As a grocer myself, I had a very personal understanding of how badly the independent store owner needed a coupon clearinghouse," he said. "Even though other companies had said there was no money to be made servicing small-volume coupon accounts, I knew that it could be done profitably."

Sarno's confidence was based on a single belief: small independent grocers would gladly pay a premium fee to a clearinghouse that gave them prompt reimbursement for their coupons. "The independent grocer operates on slim margins, so he wants to turn his money over quickly. When he takes in a hundred dollars worth of coupons, he doesn't like to wait around too long to get that money back. We figured that we could charge this grocer a bigger service fee if we offered him extra-fast reimbursement. This bigger fee would allow us to generate more money out of the low-volume account, and in so doing, we would make a profit."

Sarno developed a unique 24-hour payment plan, mailing reimbursement checks to grocers within one day after their coupons were received. By comparison, larger, established clearinghouses often took 30 days to reimburse accounts. In return for Seven Oaks' prompt turnaround, grocers allowed the clearinghouse to keep the entire eight-cents-per-coupon manufacturer's handling fee as payment. (Most clearinghouses kept only a fraction of the fee.)

"We were really the only one offering this kind of payment plan in the early days, and it was instrumental in helping us get off the ground," said Sarno. "The mom 'n pop stores liked it, because it helped their cash flow, and, with the eight-cent fee, we were able to make a profit on small-volume accounts."

Sarno created other payment options with different reimbursement schedules to offer alongside his 24-hour plan. The service fee Seven Oaks charged an account depended on two factors: the volume the account did with the company, and the payment plan it selected. High-volume accounts that waited 28 days to receive their checks were charged a much lower fee than the small store that received next-day payment.

Seven Oaks acquired plenty of experience dealing with both large and small accounts in the years following its founding. By 1986, the company, then the second-largest coupon clearinghouse behind A. C. Nielsen, counted leading supermarket chains like Waldbaum's and SuperValu among its 20,000 retail outlet customers.

These retailers mail an average of 4 million coupons a day to Seven Oaks' receiving office in El Paso, Texas. From there, the coupons are trucked across the border to the company's 140,000-square-foot processing center in Juarez, Mexico. Like almost all of its competitors in the labor-intensive coupon clearinghouse industry, Seven Oaks does all of its processing in Mexico, where wages are low by U.S. standards.

Seven Oaks entered a new field in 1981, when it started a coupon redemption agency. A redemption agency is hired by a manufacturer to keep records of, and issue payment for, all redeemed coupons turned in by a clearinghouse. Among the sixty or so manufacturers serviced by Seven Oaks' redemption agency are Thomas J. Lipton, Inc., R. T. French Co., Airwick, and MJB Coffee.

"Our redemption agency provides manufacturers with detailed statistical reports on their coupon redemptions," said Sarno. "We show them where their coupons are being returned from, so they can determine how well a promotion is working in different parts of the country."

Seven Oaks has expanded further since the mid-1980s by moving into the fulfillment field. This involves the distribution of premiums—coupons, cash, or merchandise—to consumers who respond to a manufacturer's rebate or incentive offer.

The impressive growth and expansion of Seven Oaks has made Sam Sarno a wealthy man. In 1984, his personal share of the publicly held company was estimated to be worth $4 million.[2] But the dark, squarely built company founder insists that his personality has not changed that much since his days as a neighborhood grocer.

"How does success change you? It makes your family feel

17. Seven Oaks grew rapidly, and Sarno built a large coupon processing plant in Mexico. By 1986, the company was processing over a billion coupons annually for a variety of accounts, from small "mom'n pop" stores to large chains like Waldbaum's.

more secure. It allows you to do more. But as far as changing you as a person. . . . "

Sam Sarno started life in circumstances that were conducive to such a down-to-earth attitude. Born to an Italian immigrant father and a first-generation Italian-American mother, he was raised in Cicero, Illinois—a close-knit, blue-collar community where people shared Old World roots and traditional values. After being graduated from high school, Sarno worked at a few factory jobs before being drafted into the Army in April 1941. He served as a military police officer, and, while stationed in Memphis, he met his wife, Louise.

Following his discharge from the service, Sarno and his brother-in-law opened a 3000-square-foot grocery store in the Whitehaven section of Memphis. The man who would eventually make his fortune processing coupons for grocers recalled his trepidation upon entering the grocery business.

"I didn't know pork 'n beans from Campbell soup when I started the store, and I wasn't so sure that I'd want to be a grocer for the rest of my life. But I said to myself, 'Let me try it for a year, and if I don't like it, I'll quit.'

"Well, obviously I didn't quit. I took to the business right away. Every day the grocery business presented a new challenge that forced you to think for yourself."

Sarno and his brother-in-law moved their grocery to larger storefronts several times in the late forties and early fifties, eventually acquiring a 10,000-square-foot supermarket, one of the biggest in Memphis at the time. Later, they opened a second, 18,000-square-foot location.

Like most independent grocers, the partners joined a buying co-op, Big Star, to compete with the large supermarket chains. Sam Sarno served as the head of the co-op's advertising committee, an experience that would later come into play when he began Seven Oaks.

"Through my involvement with Big Star's advertising program, I got to know people up at General Foods and other big companies. Later, when I started Seven Oaks, I called these people and told them what we were doing. They got their companies to authorize us as a clearinghouse for their coupons. Once we were authorized by those companies, all of the others followed suit, and we were quickly established as a legitimate clearinghouse."

Sarno also used his industry connections to promote Seven Oaks to potential accounts. He distributed sales literature on his new clearinghouse to the salesmen and food brokers who called on his store and asked them to pass the material along to other grocers on their routes.

"Most of my accounts in the early days were stores here in the South, because this is where the salesmen who called on my store had their other customers," he recalled. "They'd go to a store, drop off my literature, and when the owner would ask them who I was, they'd give me a good recommendation."

Sarno's ability to establish credibility for his new company was a major contributor to his ultimate success in the coupon business, where the spectre of fraud constantly haunts corporate issuers. Unscrupulous store owners have been known to pad profits by passing off bogus coupons. Corporate issuers expect clearinghouses to be their first line of defense in preventing these frauds.

Inspectors at Seven Oaks' receiving center examine coupons as they come in, looking for telltale signs of fraud. If they suspect that a batch of coupons is fraudulent, they will send it back to the store unprocessed. What signs do the fraud inspectors look for? "One thing they determine right away is whether or not the coupons in a batch are gang-cut," said Sarno. "This is when all of the coupons we receive from a particular store are cut in the same exact way. What this means is that the store owner went out and collected a bunch of newspapers and cut out the coupons himself.

"We also compare the number of coupons being redeemed by a particular store to the number being redeemed by similar stores in its market," he continued. "If a store turns in 200 of a coupon, and a store down the street turns in two of that coupon, then you've got to believe something's wrong."

If someone decides to slip two or three fraudulent coupons into a batch, Sarno concedes, there is not much a clearinghouse can do. "But if it's anything significant, we'll catch on to it. We've been in this business a long time, and we know how to look."

At 68, Sarno still maintains an active work pace at Seven Oaks. He arrives at his office every weekday morning at half past eight and remains until five, involving himself in every facet of the company's business as its chairman and CEO. After work, he likes to go bowling; his average is still in the 170 range.

"I never looked at age, not when I started the business in my fifties, and not today," he remarked. "I enjoy being involved in my work. One thing you learn in the grocery business is how to work hard; you show up at your store every day at seven and stay until seven or eight at night."

When asked what it takes to become a successful entrepreneur, Sarno listed "hard work and faith in what you're doing." Then, elaborating on the latter point: "You got to believe in your idea. That's what I did. When I started Seven Oaks, I could see the future in it."

18. *A jazz drummer by avocation and a high-tech entrepreneur by profession, Willis Drake left a group vice-presidency at Data Products Corp. in 1969 to launch Data Card Corp., maker of the first high-speed credit card encoding-embossing machine. William T. Price, a Data Card confounder, is the cornet player pictured.*

V

*Jumping
the Fence*

Robert F. de Graff *(1895–1981)*

POCKET BOOKS, INC.

"People would buy more books if they were cheaper."

It is doubtful that many readers scanning the Friday, June 16, 1939, *New York Times* noticed the small announcement buried on the bottom of page 34:

New 25¢ Books Offered

Full page ads in New York newspapers will be used to announce a new publishing plan, making available best-selling books of our time in unabridged form at 25 cents a copy, Robert F. de Graff, publisher, announced yesterday. The first ten "Pocket Books" will be put on sale today, not only through regular book channels, but also in drug and cigar stores and on newspaper stands. The books measure 4½ by 6½ inches, are printed in large type with small margins and have waterproof "Duragloss" covers.

It is even more doubtful that any of those who did bother to read the article anticipated the impact de Graff's new venture would have on America's reading habits. Within the next five years, the quiet, middle-aged, Long Island man, would sell 100

129

million Pocket Books through more than 50,000 retail outlets across the United States. In so doing, he would earn his place in publishing history as the creator of the modern American paperback industry.

De Graff was not by any means the first to market books in paperback form. Several times during the nineteenth century, enterprising publishers had experimented with paperbacks only to see them fail for lack of quality (both in the literary and production senses of the word), and lack of distribution. In England, Penguin had done well selling paperbound editions of the classics, but the few American companies who had tried publishing classics or genre fiction in paperback in the 1920s and '30s met the same fate as their counterparts in the nineteenth century.

By the time the 45-year-old de Graff launched Pocket Books in 1939, the conventional wisdom in publishing was: "The American public will not buy paperbound books." Typifying the prevailing attitude of the era was Random House founder Bennett Cerf, who told de Graff, "If by some miracle the idea of low-cost books in paper ever did go over, I'd swing my Modern Library series into paper, and Pocket Books would fold in three months."

But, of course, Pocket Books did not fold. By the time it celebrated its tenth anniversary, the company was selling 180 million paperbacks a year, making it the clear leader in what had become a large and hotly competitive market.

Although the success of Pocket Books took most people in publishing by surprise, for Robert de Graff it represented the logical extension of a 17-year career in the book business that began in 1922, when he became a salesman for the firm owned by his cousin, Nelson Doubleday. After three years in sales, de Graff was named director of Doubleday's subsidiary, The Garden City Publishing Co., which sold inexpensive reprints, primarily in cloth. During his 11-year tenure as director, de Graff created the firm's most successful imprint, Star Dollar Books, a line of nonfiction reprints.

At Garden City, de Graff became convinced that the market for reprints could be broadened if their prices were lowered and their distribution expanded beyond the normal bookstore outlets. Schoolteachers, nurses, farmers, and students, who balked at spending a dollar or two on a reprint during the Depression, would gladly part with a quarter for a smaller paperback book, he told his cousin, especially if it could be conveniently purchased at the local drugstore. But Nelson Doubleday rejected the idea of a 25-cent paperback, and, in 1936, the 41-year-old de Graff quit Garden City to start his own reprint house.

Before he could do this, however, he was persuaded to accept the presidency of Blue Ribbon Books, a house that published several lines of cloth reprints, some of which retailed for as low as 39 cents. Still, de Graff remained glued to the idea of a 25-cent mass market paperback. When he could not convince Blue Ribbon to go along with his plans for such a book, he again decided to strike out on his own.

This time, he would not be distracted by any job offers. Resigning from Blue Ribbon in February 1938, he spent a year studying the production and marketing issues involved in running a successful paperback business. Could a good-quality paperback be produced to sell for as little as 25 cents, while still allowing a publisher to make a profit? Would drugstores, newsstands, and other retail outlets that did not normally sell books be receptive to the idea of carrying paperbacks? Was the public's demand for 25-cent reprints great enough to generate the necessary sales volume?

The answer to all of these questions, de Graff discovered, was "yes." Relatively recent developments in printing technology and the availability of less costly paper would indeed make it possible to mass-produce paperbacks for between 7 and 10 cents a copy. Even after a royalty of 1 to 1.5 cents was paid to the original hardcover publisher, de Graff would be able to sell a paperback to a wholesaler for as little as 16 cents and still make a reasonable profit. This, in turn, would leave enough margin for the wholesaler and retailer to make it worthwhile for them to handle the books.

De Graff gauged the consumer demand for his paperback concept by test-marketing one title—*The Good Earth*—on a limited scale in the summer of 1938, and by mailing questionnaires to 50,000 readers. Not only did his survey convince him that people wanted inexpensive paperbacks, it also played a role in shaping their famous pocket-sized format.

Discussing the survey in a later interview, de Graff recalled that its results proved two things: "That people would buy more books if they were cheaper; and, that most people didn't have enough time to read. That's where I got the idea for the size of my books. I thought if I could make them of a size that would easily slip into a pocket or a handbag, people would carry them around and read them whenever they had a few free minutes. The trade name [Pocket Books] then came easily."

Interestingly, a second survey of Pocket Books customers taken by de Graff in the fall of 1941, a little over two years after the company was founded, proved the accuracy of his prediction in convincing fashion. The answers he received revealed that Pocket Books readers represented a cross-section of average Americans who bought paperbacks because of their low price, convenient size, and widespread availability. Those responding to the survey had been buying about a quarter of the three to fifty books they read a year, but now were purchasing a yearly average of twenty-five Pocket Books.

But even the optimistic de Graff could not have anticipated this kind of acceptance when he founded Pocket Books in 1939. After discussing his paperback idea with a friend, Richard Simon, of Simon & Schuster, de Graff dropped his plan to start a company in an uncertain field on his own. Instead, he agreed to form a partnership with Simon, Max Schuster, and another Simon & Schuster partner, Leon Shimkin. Under the terms of the agreement, de Graff owned a 51 percent share of the new company and was named as its president, while the remaining share was divided among the other partners.

"Mr. de Graff felt that he wanted some help in handling the administrative end of his new company," recalled Leon Shimkin, a warm and intelligent man now in his eighties. "This was a wise decision on his part, because his greatest strength was in marketing and in gauging the paperback sales potential of a hardcover title. He wasn't well-versed in corporate management, and he recognized this fact."

In May 1939, Pocket Books was officially started with $30,000. Its offices consisted of a windowless two-room suite at Simon & Schuster's headquarters on Fourth Avenue and were staffed by de Graff, a salesman named Pete Howe, and two other employees. Its original "list" consisted of ten titles selected by de Graff: *Lost Horizon, Topper,* and *Wuthering Heights* (all chosen because they had been recently made into successful movies); *The Murder of Roger Ackroyd,* by Agatha Christie (to test the mystery market); *The*

Bridge of San Luis Rey (a recent Pulitzer Prize–winner); *Bambi* (a proven children's favorite); *Enough Rope,* by Dorothy Parker (poetry by a well-known figure); *Wake Up and Live* (a popular self-help book); *The Way of All Flesh,* by English novelist Samuel Butler (a satiric portrait of Victorian life that was regarded as a classic); and *Five Great Tragedies by Shakespeare* (hopefully a perennial seller to students).

Although they shared his enthusiasm, de Graff's partners did not share his unguarded optimism when the first Pocket Books hit the market in June. This became obvious when the foursome wrote the copy for their introductory newspaper ad: "Out today—The new Pocket Books that may revolutionize New York's reading habits." Years later, de Graff would recall, "We had a little argument over the ad. I wanted to say 'will revolutionize' . . . but everybody seemed to feel that was too strong, so we compromised on 'may.' "

This cautiousness was also evident in the partners' original marketing plan: to print an average of only 10,000 copies of each title and to sell Pocket Books only in New York. "You have to remember that this was a completely new idea at the time," recalled Leon Shimkin. "We were all very confident, but we wanted to see how the idea went over before we made a full commitment."

If the partners needed concrete proof of the paperback's sales potential, it was certainly provided by Pocket Books' early performance. In his authoritative work, *A History of Book Publishing in the United States,* John Tebbel writes, "The big New York bookstores Brentano's, Putnam's and Scribner's had each taken 100 copies on a return basis. Other outlets were much more optimistic, however. Macy's took 10,000 copies; Liggett's drugstore in Grand Central Station 5000; and Union News, a large quantity for its stands all over New York. . . . The first reorder came from a bookstore, Doubleday's shop in Grand Central Station, and another, Concord Books, reordered 1000 copies. A small cigar stand near the Pocket Books office sold 110 copies in the first day and a half, and Macy's reported 695 copies sold on the first day, even before the books went into its windows."[1]

Within two months, a flood of telegrammed orders from other cities forced Pocket Books to begin national distribution. Initially, the company relied on a field staff of seventy-eight book representatives to sell its paperbacks, but it soon realized that widespread distribution could be achieved more effectively through magazine wholesalers. By 1945, Pocket Books had reduced its field staff to fifteen supervisors, who oversaw 712 magazine wholesalers, who distributed the paperbacks to 75,000 stores in the U.S. and Canada.

By developing this extensive distribution network, Pocket Books achieved a level of market saturation never before known in the book industry. For the first time, readers in small towns that did not have bookstores could purchase a fairly current title simply by visiting their local drugstore. Even in big cities, the new paperbacks made a difference: in 1943 there were about a dozen outlets for hardcover originals in Detroit, compared to over 1200 for Pocket Books.

Robert de Graff relied on more than a low price and massive distribution to sell Pocket Books to the public. An astute merchandiser, he pioneered the paperback display rack, supplying retailers with $1.5 million of rack equipment during his company's first decade.

Another de Graff innovation was the slick, colorful paperback cover. Wanting to create a book that was "pleasing to the eye and agreeable to the touch," he used red end sheets for Pocket Books pages and semi-stiff cardboard with a glossy sheen of laminated cellulose acetate, called Perma-Gloss, for covers. The covers themselves were vividly illustrated, often depicting scenes that looked more like a movie poster than a book jacket. Although they offended some publishing purists, the colorful covers attracted attention on store racks. "Mr. de Graff saw covers as a merchandising tool, and the rest of us shared this view," said Leon Shimkin.

In November 1944, Pocket Books was purchased for $3 million by Chicago department store heir Marshall Field III, who also owned four radio stations, the *Chicago Sun*, the Quarrie Corp. (a reference book publisher), *PM* newspaper in New York, and the Sunday newspaper supplement *Parade*. Robert de Graff continued to serve as president of the company after the sale, leaving the office in 1949 to become chairman of the board. Leon Shimkin, who succeeded de Graff as president, bought Pocket Books back from Field's estate in 1957 for $5 million and later merged the company with Simon & Schuster (which also had been owned by Field).

Robert de Graff gradually became less involved with Pocket Books during the 1950s. By the time the company had celebrated its 25th anniversary in 1964 with the sale of its 300 millionth book, its founder had retired to his Long Island estate, where he devoted much of his time to various philanthropies.

Ironically, the man who changed the reading habits of millions of Americans was not much of a reader himself. "I have never known him to read a book for pleasure, but rarely have I seen him err in judging the sales potential of a book," one of de Graff's early associates is quoted by author John Tebbel.

Tall and blond with a long, angular face, de Graff was born to a prosperous Plainfield, New Jersey, family. For a time it seemed as if he would live a life of idle leisure. After graduating from Hotchkiss, he skipped college and devoted most of his time to his favorite hobby, collecting automobiles. He served as a lieutenant in World War I, and for four years after the war he dabbled at a variety of casual jobs. Then, at 27, he entered publishing, dramatically altering the course of his life and that of the industry.

Willis K. Drake (1923-   )

DATA CARD CORPORATION

"Support good ideas with a solid corporate structure."

As a director of the Minnesota Cooperation Office, a private nonprofit group devoted to helping new businesses get started in the state, Willis ("Bill") Drake is often called upon to counsel would-be entrepreneurs. Invariably, his advice includes this message: *Every good idea needs a solid corporate plan to be turned into a successful business.*

"The biggest mistake that new entrepreneurs make is that they fail to visualize the entire corporate structure that will be needed to make their idea work," observed the retired Data Card Corporation founder. "They tend to be biased in favor of their own experience; if they are marketers they overemphasize marketing, if they are engineers they overemphasize engineering. They don't cover all the bases when developing their corporate plans, and this often kills their ideas before they get off the ground."

Bill Drake had both a good idea and the solid corporate plan needed to turn it into a reality in 1969, when, at 47, he started Data Card Corp. on one million dollars capital. A Minneapolis-based company, Data Card makes equipment that embosses credit cards (producing the raised letters and numbers on their fronts) and encodes the magnetic strips on their backs with computer-readable information. Data Card's machinery embossed and encoded over 90 percent of the roughly one billion credit cards and

bank machine cards in circulation worldwide in 1986. This accounted for the bulk of the company's $153.5 million revenues,
but Data Card also did a healthy business selling blank plastic
cards as well as machines that automatically insert cards in stiff
paper sleeves for mailing.

Data Card might never have grown to attain this level of success, said Drake, had not he assembled a professional management team *before* he launched the company. "A lot of entrepreneurs are contemptuous of managers. They adopt the attitude,
'What do I need an accountant for? I have a good idea and the
start-up capital, so I'm ready to go.' Fortunately, I didn't fall into
this trap when I started Data Card. My first three employees were
senior management people: Dick Hencley, a mechanical engineer whose expertise was in manufacturing; Bill Price, a commercial banker who specialized in finance; and Tom Deere, an
executive with experience in marketing. When you added my experience in engineering and administration to the group's, you
had a team that collectively was capable of managing a $100 mil-
lion corporation."

A deliberate, soft-spoken man with intense cobalt blue eyes,
Bill Drake learned the value of corporate planning early in his
career, when he took a job as a technical writer for Engineering
Research Associates (ERA), a pioneering computer company. ERA
was formed in 1946 by a group of brilliant young engineers who
had worked on code-breaking and communications systems for
the U.S. Navy during World War II.

"The Navy wanted to see the group stay together after the
war, because it recognized the potential importance of what they
were doing," explained Drake. "It encouraged the group to form
ERA and promised to give them a certain amount of work.

"I joined ERA in 1947, after graduating from Purdue. Looking back, I can see that it was one of those 'accidents' that happen
in your life that change its course forever. I thought I was just
taking a job with a small company, but I wound up being in the
middle of one of the most exciting technological developments
of all time. ERA was one of the two major centers of what turned
out to be the computer industry. Out of it, at least in part, came
the first commercial computer."

Like a former athlete recalling teammates from a long-ago
championship season, Bill Drake still glows with affection when

he describes the camaraderie at ERA. "Everyone was wildly excited about what we were doing, and we all shared a basic feeling that nothing was impossible. There was no red tape and no politics; it was a fantastic place and naive beyond belief. We had one very big customer standing behind us, so we didn't need to know anything about business."

Drake made many lifelong friends and professional contacts at ERA, and his experience there taught him a valuable lesson about persistence that would later pay off when he developed his embossing-encoding machine. But he was not blind to the company's faults. The special relationship with the Navy could not be expected to last forever, and Drake realized that ERA would have to implement tighter management controls and develop products with at least some commercial application if it were going to survive. Or, to put it in Bill Drake's current parlance: ERA had to "support good ideas with a solid corporate structure."

Drake tried to persuade ERA's management to market peripheral gear to the small companies that were beginning to make one-of-a-kind computing machines for specialized applications. But the proposal was turned down by ERA, which was content to continue doing customized work for the Navy and a select group of other customers.

Convinced that ERA was jeopardizing its future by refusing to develop commercial products, Drake left the company in 1950 and took a job with Lear, Inc. One year later he was invited back to ERA, which had revised its strategy and started a commercial products program. During Drake's absence, the company had developed the ERA 1103, one of the two first high-speed general-purpose computers. (The other was the UNIVAC One machine built by Philadelphia's Eckert-Mauchly Computer Corporation.)

In on the ground floor of the computer industry, ERA could have emerged as an IBM-level giant, but the research-oriented company still lacked the corporate infrastructure to take advantage of its pioneering product. Unable to market its computer effectively, ERA was sold in December 1951 to Remington Rand, the business machine maker that had also acquired Eckert-Mauchly.

Under Remington Rand's ownership, the ERA 1103 was marketed as a scientific computer, while the UNIVAC One, which was geared for a higher-volume input and output, was developed as the first commercial business computer. In 1953, the company installed the first UNIVAC at the new General Electric (GE) major appliance plant in Louisville, Kentucky. Willis Drake, who, along with the rest of the ERA staff, had remained with the company after the sale, was sent to the GE plant as Remington Rand's account representative.

"I lived in Louisville for about two-and-a-half years, working with UNIVAC," he said. "It was complete chaos down there; no one knew what they were doing, because we had no precedents to go by. This was the first commercial computer application, and we were traveling through uncharted territory."

The UNIVAC One was bulky, slow, and highly unreliable by modern computer standards. It had 13,000 vacuum tubes, and its internal memory consisted of an erratic mercury magnetic delay line. "We ended up having 13 full-time service engineers there just trying to make the system run," recalled Drake. "The machine couldn't run for more than a couple of hours at a time, and it was always breaking down. It took about two years before the system finally became operational."

Compounding UNIVAC's technological problems was the constant bickering and infighting that occurred within the Remington Rand organization. "A lack of leadership on the part of Remington Rand plagued UNIVAC One from the start," said Drake. "There was never good communication within the company, and backroom politicking was always getting in the way of constructive problem-solving. The traditional business machine people regarded the new computer as a threat and did their best to sabotage it."

The Remington Rand experience taught Drake a valuable lesson in the importance of maintaining a solid corporate management structure. Had the company's management been better able to control the divisive factions within the organization and establish clearly defined chains of command, then it, and not IBM, might have come to dominate the computer industry.

But Bill Drake was not thinking about the broader implications of the Remington fiasco in 1957, when he and other ERA alumni resigned from the troubled company (then called Sperry-Rand as a result of a merger two years earlier). The engineers rallied around the man who had been their acknowledged leader

139

at ERA, Bill Norris, who, after being pushed out of UNIVAC, was starting his own computer company, Control Data. (See profile on page 112.)

"I went to work for Control Data at half my previous salary," said Drake. "My first job was to raise $600,000 in start-up capital that we decided we needed. We planned to do this through the public issue of 600,000 one-dollar shares of stock. This was an unprecedented concept; we proposed to sell shares in a company that had no product, no facility, and no assets—just an idea and a solid business plan."

Bill Drake conducted presentations at his home at night for potential investors. Despite the unorthodox nature of the offering, he more than doubled the original stock issue, selling 1.4 million shares in only three nights. The value of Control Data stock soared in the coming years, greatly increasing the wealth of all investors—including Drake, who purchased 12,500 shares with mostly borrowed money.

Encouraged by his success at raising start-up capital for Control Data, Drake left the company in 1958 to start Midwest Technical Development Corporation, "the first publicly owned venture capital firm." Although the company did well for a time, providing seed money to a number of successful high-tech ventures, it eventually faltered and closed in 1962.

"That was the low point of my career," said Drake. "I lost most of my money in the venture capital firm, and I didn't know what to do. So, like everyone else who doesn't know what to do, I became a consultant."

One of Drake's clients was a fellow ERA alumnus, Erwin Tomash, head of Data Products, a manufacturer of OEM computer peripherals. "Data Products was considering getting into end-user peripherals, and they wanted me to study the potential market," said Drake. "I told them it looked very good, so they said, 'Well, if it looks so good, why don't you come and head our end-user product program?'"

In 1964, Drake became a group vice-president at Data Products in charge of the end-user products division. About three years later, the company acquired the rights to a proposed credit card embosser that was to be controlled by computer tape. "No other embosser then on the market was computer-compatible," he said. "Other embossers were controlled by paper tape, punch cards, or key strokes. Our proposed machine would receive its instructions from computer tape. This would represent a significant improvement in terms of speed and accuracy."

After more than a year of trying, however, Data Products' engineers were unable to develop a workable prototype of the new embosser. The company was ready to drop the machine and concentrate on more proven products, but Drake continued to press for a solution to the embosser's mechanical problems.

Finally, in 1969, he resigned from Data Products and, with financial backing from the company, formed Data Card Corp. to continue work on the embossing machine. Seven months later, Drake's engineers developed a workable model of the embosser.

In addition to being computer-compatible, the new embosser represented another major advance over previous designs: instead of rotating heavy metal type dies to emboss each character, as other machines did, the new "Data Card 1500" moved the lighter plastic card and kept type dies stationary. This greatly reduced the amount of downtime associated with embossers and (together with the computerized controls) resulted in a machine that embossed cards five times faster than its nearest rival.

Data Card shipped its first order, two machines to American Express, in late 1970. "American Express initially wanted us to give them a machine for free, saying that if they used the machine and endorsed it, then we would be flooded with orders from other credit card companies," recounted Drake. "But I always believed that once you start giving away your product, you're headed for trouble. We told American Express that they would have to pay the same price as everyone else."

In 1970, that price was $160,000 per machine. One year later, Data Card introduced a new $250,000 model that could encode as well as emboss cards. The company continued to bring out new models during the remainder of the decade, as the ever-expanding credit card boom sent the demand for embosser-encoders soaring. Data Card's earnings increased 30 to 50 percent a year between 1970 and 1978, when sales passed $44 million.

As Bill Drake had anticipated, the company's professional management team handled this growth smoothly and efficiently, guiding Data Card into new products like labeling tags, and opening new markets through subsidiaries in England, France, and Germany.

Retired as Data Card CEO since 1981, Drake offered this perspective on his post-40 career: "I believe it was better for me to start after 40. When you're younger, your efforts in business are strictly 'amateur's night'; you try to overpower all obstacles with sheer energy. But when you're older, you do things in a more systematic way."

Wilbert L. Gore *(1912–)*

W. L. GORE & ASSOCIATES, INC.

"We don't manage people here—they manage themselves."

"Here, there is no need for bosses, assignment of tasks, establishing lines of command, and the like. The necessary functions are organized by voluntary commitments and universal agreement on the objective."

This sounds more like a dreamer's vision of a utopian commune than it does an American centimillionaire's description of his international corporation. But Wilbert "Bill" Gore is no ordinary corporate founder, and his W. L. Gore & Associates, Inc., is no ordinary company.

A major manufacturer of synthetic fibers, including the famous Gore-tex laminate that is used in everything from sportswear and tents to astronaut suits and artificial heart valves, W. L. Gore is a highly unstructured company, even by the open standards of the high-tech industry. The Newark, Delaware, firm has no ranks, no titles, and none of the other "authoritarian constraints" that characterize traditional corporations.

In their place is a "lattice organization," devised by Gore, in which each associate (no one is called an employee) is allowed to create his or her own job description.

"We don't manage people here—they manage themselves," explained the compact, craggy-faced entrepreneur. "We don't try to fit an associate into a slot. It's up to every associate to find a

143

job that will be enjoyable and will contribute to the success of the company."

Associates join together in "teams" to work on special projects and perform routine tasks. The teams set their own goals, and although there are no appointed bosses, "natural leaders" evolve, according to Gore, based on "knowledge, skill, courage, enthusiasm, dominance, dedication, historical situations, and other nonobjective and perhaps mystical factors."

Gore's unorthodox management system is not without its problems. He concedes that newcomers to his company sometimes take a while to adjust to the freedom of its lattice organization. "Most people are raised in authoritarian situations; their parents were authority figures for them at home, their teachers in school. They're used to being told what to do, and when they come here their attitude is 'Tell me what to do' or 'Tell me what you expect from me.' There's an adjustment that they have to make to the lattice system."

But this problem is more than made up for, according to Gore, by the stimulating effect that the lattice system has on those employees who do adjust. "Hierarchical structures stifle freedom and creativity. People will be tremendously productive and innovative when they are given the opportunity to exercise their talents freely. Our associates are probably twice as productive and three times as creative as people in other companies because they have more freedom."

An Idaho native who speaks in a slow, deliberate cadence that sounds vaguely like that of Ronald Reagan, Gore acquired both his devotion to the lattice management style and his expertise in synthetic fibers during his 17 years as a research chemist with DuPont. During the latter part of his career, he was a member of a special task force appointed to explore new commercial uses for a polymer that DuPont had patented years earlier as polytetrafluoroethylene (PTFE) or, as it would later be called, "Teflon." The task force drew together twenty researchers from different departments, all working as equals toward a common goal with minimal interference from management. Years later, Bill Gore would remember it as one of his best experiences at DuPont.

"The task force was exciting, challenging, and, most of all, fun," he recalled. "We worked very hard, and everyone pulled together. It seemed like such a good way to structure a work environment. I began to wonder why entire companies couldn't be run the same way."

Gore's task force was disbanded in 1957, after another DuPont group discovered a new method of fabricating PTFE. But the research chemist remained fascinated by the polymer, convinced that it would make an ideal insulation for electrical computer wires if it could be made more flexible. Taking a supply of PTFE home to his basement laboratory, Gore began experimenting with it at night and on weekends.

In September, he succeeded in developing a "PTFE ribbon cable" that had the necessary flexibility. For months he tried to convince DuPont to add the insulator to its product line, but the company refused, preferring to concentrate its marketing efforts on "plastic raw materials" rather than on finished products like Gore's cable.

His proposal rejected, Gore considered leaving DuPont to start his own business manufacturing the ribbon cable. But he was 45 years old with two children in college and three more in high school; his salary was good, his position in the company secure, his chance of receiving a big promotion excellent. Everything and everyone told him to stay.

Except his wife, Vieve.

"It was a bit scary, but I was all for Bill leaving DuPont," recalled Vieve Gore. "I said to him, 'Look, if you don't try this, you will always be sorry. Let's give it two years. If you do fall on your face, you can dust yourself off and DuPont will take you back.'"

On New Year's Day, 1958, Bill and Vieve Gore's twenty-third wedding anniversary, Bill's resignation from DuPont became official, and W. L. Gore & Associates was born. The only "associate" was Vieve Gore, who handled the administrative end of the business while her husband made ribbon cables in his basement laboratory with PTFE purchased from DuPont. Start-up capital was $100,000, the couple's entire life savings—enough to keep them afloat for two years if the business failed.

The business started slowly, but orders for the insulating cable gradually trickled in. The Gores' big break came when the city of Denver ordered $100,000 worth of cables for its water monitoring system. "That is what put us over the hump," recalled Bill Gore.

145

By the time their two-year trial period was over, the Gores had twenty-five associates working three shifts. The business was still operating out of the Gores' basement, but, as Vieve Gore noted, "things were beginning to spill over into our yard."

The couple acquired their first real plant, a building on Newark's Paper Mill Road, in 1960, just in time for the computer revolution. The rapid advance of computer technology and the resultant "computerization" of virtually every corner of industry, sent the demand for Gore's insulators spiraling. By the middle of the decade, over two hundred associates were working at Gore's Newark plant to keep up with the ever-increasing volume of orders.

Although the company was doing well financially, somewhere along the line the camaraderie of the basement-lab era was lost; gaping holes were beginning to appear in Gore's lattice system.

"I was walking through the plant one summer day when it suddenly struck me that I no longer knew everyone's name," recalled Gore. "The atmosphere around the plant was different; people were referring to the company as 'they,' not 'us.' There wasn't the same kind of feeling we had in the early years."

After analyzing the situation, the Gores concluded that the problem lay in the number of people employed at the plant. "The lattice system could not work in a plant that got too big," explained Bill Gore. "We therefore decided that it would be better to have many smaller facilities than fewer large ones."

The Gores opened a second plant in Flagstaff, Arizona, in 1967, providing them with a chance to test their theory and reach the expanding western market at the same time. Shifting some of their production to Arizona, they reduced the number of associates at the Newark plant to one hundred fifty. The results were what the Gores had expected; the atmosphere improved dramatically.

Since that time, the Gores have made it a policy to limit the number of associates employed at any one facility to two hundred. Today, the privately held Gore company has thirty-five plants in the U.S., Europe, and Japan—all of them adhering to the two hundred associate limit.

The most famous product produced at these plants is Gore-tex, a razor-thin membrane that is both "breathable" and waterproof. Gore-tex contains billions of microscopic pores per square inch. These pores are wide enough to allow the free flow of air, yet small enough to prevent the passage of water molecules. Because of this property, Gore-tex has gained widespread acceptance among manufacturers of sportswear and outdoor apparel, who laminate it to their fabrics creating garments that are weatherproof without being hot and uncomfortable to wear.

Gore-tex was invented by the Gores' oldest son, Bob, a Ph.D. chemical engineer, in the fall of 1969, after a long, painstaking effort. For some time, the Gores had realized that PTFE could be developed into a unique, "breathable" material if its layers of molecules could be unfolded. To do this, Bill and Bob Gore tried heating rods of the polymer to different temperatures, then gently stretching them. But regardless of how carefully they pulled, the material would inevitably snap before it stretched very far. Then, one evening, in a fit of frustration, Bob Gore yanked a rod of PTFE from the oven and pulled at it violently. To his surprise, the one-foot rod stretched the entire length of his extended arms.

Although Bob Gore's discovery would become the basis for a $250 million business, Gore-tex's early history was far from trouble-free. Bill and Vieve Gore conducted the first field test of the product in the summer of 1970, when they took a homemade Gore-tex tent on their annual camping trip to Wind River, Wyoming. On their first night out, it rained, and, after feeling around the inside of the porous tent, the Gores were pleased to discover it was bone dry. Then it started to hail, and the ice tore tiny holes in the top of the tent, filling it with water. "We certainly didn't sleep well that night," said Bill Gore.

The experience taught the Gores that their new product, though waterproof, would have to be made stronger if it was going to be marketed as a weatherproofing laminate. But even after the necessary strength was added, Gore-tex still faced problems. Early Gore-tex jackets and running apparel were so thick and heavy, they almost stood up by themselves. Far more serious was the tendency of the Gore-tex membrane to weaken and allow water molecules to pass through when it was exposed to certain oils which are present in perspiration. The discovery of this problem prompted the company to recall all noninsulated Gore-tex apparel.

In late 1979, Bob Gore restructured the molecular configu-

19. Bill and Vieve Gore enjoying themselves on one of their many trips. The couple's most incredible journey began on New Year's Day 1958 (their twenty-third wedding anniversary) when Bill officially resigned from his position at DuPont to start W. L. Gore & Associates. Together, the Gores built the business from a basement chemical shop to a $200 million-plus corporation that makes a wide range of fiber products, including the famous laminate Gore-tex.

ration of the Gore-tex membrane, making it impervious to perspiration oils. Other refinements allowed the membrane to be laminated on softer, more comfortable fabrics. As a result, the number of manufacturers using the Gore-tex fabric laminate jumped from six in the mid-1970s to 125 in 1982.

Almost a decade before Gore-tex had been fully accepted by sportswear makers, Bill Gore had succeeded in opening a market for the polymer membrane in the medical supply industry. This began with a 1971 ski vacation in Vail that the Gores took with a group of friends, including Dr. Ben Eiseman of Denver General Hospital.

"One morning I pulled this tubing out of my pocket and asked, 'Ben, do you think this would be any good as an artificial vein or artery?'" said Gore. "He took the tube and asked what it was, and I explained that it was expanded Teflon. Then he said, 'Let me have it, and I'll put it in a pig.' A few weeks later he called me back and was all excited because he'd put it in a pig and it was working fine."

By 1985, more than a million people had Gore-tex medical products in their bodies, primarily vascular grafts for arteries and artificial knee ligaments. "Gore-tex is an ideal bio-compatible material, because it's not rejected by the body," explained

Gore. "The patient's natural tissue grows into its open pore spaces, so the body doesn't identify Gore-tex as a foreign object."

The Gores have shared the wealth created by the success of Gore-tex with their associates. They put 15 percent of all profits into a pool that is distributed to associates twice a year. They also have an Associates' Stock Ownership Plan (ASOP) that places company stock equivalent to 15 percent of an associate's salary into a retirement fund.

Money, however, is not the primary motivator of Gore associates. When discussing the benefits of their jobs, they use terms like "maximum freedom," "opportunities for growth," and "personal fulfillment."

But Bill Gore has never been one to dismiss the importance of money, for his company or its associates. "It is crucial that we make money and have fun doing it. Actually, making money is a creative activity; it means that people are applauding you for making a good contribution."

20. *Anthony Rossi (left) and Ed Price stand by one of Tropicana's transportation innovations, the "Great White Train" commissioned in 1970 to carry Florida orange juice to northern cities.*

VI

Making It Happen

Murray J. Harpole *(1921–)*

PENTAIR, INC.

"I decided ... I would give it five years no matter how tough it got."

When Murray Harpole tells of the perils he encountered after founding Pentair, Inc., a manufacturer of diversified paper products, in 1966, one is reminded of the camper who has narrowly escaped a bear attack. Once the threat has been long removed, the joy of recounting the near-catastrophe can be savored over and over again.

In Harpole's case, the tale of Pentair's early tribulations is especially harrowing, since the odds against the Minnesota company's surviving—let alone gaining a berth on the Fortune 500 list—seemed overwhelming. A 44-year-old electromechanical engineer, Harpole had gone into business with four partners to manufacture high-altitude balloons and related instrumentation for government research. The group, formerly co-workers at Litton Industries in Minneapolis–St. Paul, named their venture "Pent" (because there were five of them) · "air" (with an atmosphere-bound product). They started the company when an opportunity arose to take over several government contracts from Litton, after their former employer decided that it was no longer interested in making balloons.

What the fivesome hadn't anticipated was the escalation of the Vietnam War. Shortly after they pooled their $25,000 capital and rented a building, President Johnson announced that he was cutting back on atmospheric research and rechanneling the funds

153

to guns and ammunition for Southeast Asia. "The announcement came at the end of the government's fiscal year on June 30—just a week before our scheduled start-up date of July 6," Harpole recalled. Before it had made or sold a single balloon, Pentair saw the market for its product disappear.

Despite the loss of their only customer, the five partners remained determined to build a successful business. "We agreed we'd do whatever was necessary to get the company off the ground," said Harpole, "even if this meant changing our plan for atmospheric balloons and manufacturing an entirely different product."

Harpole's decision to continue onward was part of a commitment he had made to himself and his family. After 20 years of working as an engineer for large companies like Honeywell and Litton, he had grown tired of the corporate routine. Many nights, he had lain awake talking to his wife, Ruth, about his desire to strike out on his own.

"We agreed that if I was going to start a business, I should commit myself to it for a predetermined amount of time. So I decided when we started the company that I would give it five years, no matter how tough it got.

"The only way I'd quit was if we ran out of money completely, because then you have no choice. But short of that, you say to yourself, this is the only thing I'm going to think about or work on for the next five years. You put all your savings into it, your children's college education money, and everything else. I told my four kids [ages 16, 14, 11 and 6], 'You may have to fund your own way through college.'"

For Harpole, the gamble paid off. By the mid-1980s, Pentair had become a leading manufacturer of paper for the printing, packaging, and business forms industries. Its $545 million in annual sales earned it a ranking of 440th on the Fortune 500 list in 1985. Today, paper produced by Pentair is used for everything from the *Encyclopedia Brittanica* and the *New Yorker* magazine to single-service sugar pouches, Mr. Coffee coffee filters, and U.S. postage stamps.

The paper business wasn't the second—or even the third— choice of Pentair's founders after the collapse of their balloon-making venture. "We were strictly opportunistic. We were willing to try anything that looked feasible," remarked Harpole, a compact, gray-haired man who speaks in a matter-of-fact monotone.

Before it could find a replacement for its ill-fated balloon business, however, Pentair faced a more basic problem—how to raise the capital it needed to survive. "It became evident that the $25,000 we had pooled as a partnership wasn't going to be enough to see us through, so we decided to raise money by going public."

In August 1966, Pentair issued 200,000 shares of stock at $1 per share. By the end of the year the company, still without a product to manufacture, had managed to sell the entire $200,000 offering, mostly to individuals who had no great wealth. "The established, sophisticated investor had no interest in us," said Harpole. "The people who bought our stock were mechanics, secretaries, gas station attendants, and others of average means. They could ill afford to lose money on an investment. We had an obligation to these investors to get our company off to a successful start."

With this goal in mind, Harpole and his associates bought a struggling manufacturer of plastic canoes which was located in their building complex. Although they knew nothing about the plastic boat business, Pentair's founders bought the canoe company because "it was available and the price was right." The partners succeeded in putting the operation back in the black, but they soon discovered that canoes would not be an answer to their cash flow problems. Explained Harpole: "You build canoes in the winter, ship them in the spring, and don't get paid for them until the summer."

Pentair also struck out with its second acquisition, a fringe-leather jacket and moccasin firm in Spooner, Wisconsin. The owners, a couple undergoing marital difficulties, were willing to unload cheaply, even though fringed Indian wear was a fashion rage at the time. But shortly after Pentair bought the business, the fringe-leather fad peaked out, leaving the company with a large unsold inventory.

By this time, three of the original partners had become discouraged enough to drop out, and a fourth had died, leaving Harpole to run the company alone. Two years into his five-year commitment, with only $10,000 remaining in the coffers, the

21. Murray J. Harpole, founder of Pentair, started his company to make high-altitude balloons, then tried making plastic canoes, before finally achieving success in the paper business.

middle-aged engineer came back for a third try—the one that would eventually make him rich. On June 3, 1968, he purchased a foundering Ladysmith, Wisconsin, paper mill that manufactured single-ply toilet tissue. Harpole assumed the mill's $1.5 million debt and agreed to pay its owner $10,000 down and another $20,000 at the end of the year, plus five percent of after-tax profits for the following five years.

Despite the mill's financial problems, Murray Harpole was confident that he could turn it into a profitable venture. "The mill's people knew how to make a product, and they were selling it, so they obviously knew how to make it well enough to satisfy a customer. They just weren't making any money at it. All we had to figure out was not how to make paper—but how to make the operation profitable."

As an experienced engineer, Harpole was able to improve the mill's efficiency and trim production costs within months. By the end of the year, he had the operation running smoothly enough to land his first big order, a three-year contract with Procter & Gamble to make absorbent paper wadding for its new Pampers disposable diapers.

"The contract was for only three years, since P&G expected to be using a new technological process after that, so the big paper companies didn't want it," Harpole explained. "But we viewed it as a badly needed reprieve from our cash flow problems."

With money flowing into Pentair's coffers, at least temporarily, Harpole began casting about for other acquisitions. In 1969, he purchased a second paper mill in Trinidad, but was forced to shut it down a short time later after a violent insurrection on the island.

Nevertheless, the unsuccessful Trinidad venture brought Pentair valuable media attention. The company had received some publicity from the Pampers contract, and after the Trinidad acquisition it became the subject of stories in the trade press, which described it as "a small company that was going international." This notoriety created a new level of interest in the company on the part of investors; Pentair's stock shot up from $2 to $25 and split three-for-one. Using this new-found backing from the financial community, Harpole acquired a larger paper mill in Niagara, Wisconsin, in 1972.

The Niagara mill, formerly owned by Kimberly-Clark, produced groundwood paper, used in the magazine publishing industry. Like most of the businesses bought by Harpole, it was losing money at the time of the acquisition, operating only four days a week.

The problem was not with the mill itself, but with the magazine industry, which was experiencing the worst depression in its history. With venerable periodicals like *Look* and *Life* ceasing publication, and most other magazines suffering a decline in circulation, the market for groundwood paper had gone soft. TV had steadily eaten into the advertising base of national periodicals over the previous two decades. Not only did TV hold magnetic sway over audiences, but with broadcast channels in every market, local businesses could use it as an advertising medium, something they could not do with a nationally distributed magazine. Many industry members believed that the general interest magazine would go the way of the dinosaur, taking much of the market for groundwood paper with it.

This prediction could not have been more wrong. After falling to its nadir in the early 1970s, the magazine industry made a dramatic comeback, spurred by the use of computers, which made it possible to include regional advertising sections in na-

tional publications. Around the same time, another trend occurred that had a rejuvenating effect on the periodical market—
the rise of special-interest magazines. New publications devoted
to everything from doll collecting to van customizing began ap-
pearing, each claiming a small, but loyal, group of readers. Collectively, they helped push the demand for groundwood paper
to new heights.

For once in its corporate life, Pentair, Inc. was at the right
place at the right time. "We acquired the Niagara mill on April
3, 1972," said Harpole, who has instant recall of important dates
in his life. "By August we were running full production, seven
days a week. By the end of the year, it was a seller's market.

"I'd like to be able to claim that we bought the groundwood
mill because we foresaw the comeback of magazines, but that's
just not true. It was largely a matter of good luck." As one who
has seen his share of luck of both varieties, Harpole added, "If
you work hard, the odds are that more good things will happen
to you than bad."

By the end of 1972, one year past his five-year deadline, Harpole had brought Pentair to the point where for the first time
since starting the business, its survival was no longer in doubt.
"Before that, it was questionable," he admitted. "But now, we'd
established a meaningful presence in the paper industry and we
felt we had the potential for becoming a stable, long-term operation."

Pentair acquired three additional paper companies in Ohio,
Wisconsin, and Michigan over the next decade. In the 1980s, it
has diversified into tool and machinery manufacturing, buying
the Porter-Cable Corporation of Jackson, Tennessee, and Delta
International Machinery Corporation of Pittsburgh.

In making all of its acquisitions, Pentair has adhered to the
same formula: to seek out underperforming, undervalued companies that can be turned around through efficient management.
"We substitute sweat equity for dollars," explained Harpole.

This approach was born out of necessity back in the days
when Pentair was strapped for capital, but Murray Harpole is not
one to change a successful formula; he still buys underperforming properties and still keeps the company's management aus-
terely lean at the top. At Pentair's corporate headquarters, a
rented seventh floor in an older office building in suburban St.

Paul, there are only twenty-eight employees, most of them clerical (out of a corporatewide total of 4800).

"Up until 1976 or so, our corporate office consisted of three or four people; we couldn't afford any more. Without a large corporate staff, each of our operating units had a high degree of autonomy, so they developed entrepreneurial attitudes that led to innovation and growth," Harpole explained.

In November 1985, Harpole departed from his original growth-through-acquisition strategy when he entered into a joint agreement with Minnesota Power Corporation to construct a $400 million paper mill in Duluth. This marks the first time that Pentair will actually build, rather than acquire, a production facility. When completed in 1988, the mill will be the world's largest maker of the super-calendared paper that is used in newspaper inserts, catalogs, and direct mail flyers.

Murray Harpole, however, will not be in command when the new mill opens. On October 31, 1986, his 65th birthday, he retired from Pentair and is no longer connected with the St. Paul firm in an official capacity.

The Minnesota entrepreneur, who clung tenaciously to his five-year plan when he started Pentair, has equally strong ideas about when a company founder should step down and turn over the reins of power to younger management.

"Mandatory retirement at 65 should be a policy at all corporations," Harpole declared. "In order to maintain an enthusiastic and committed work force, the people at all levels of a company have to know that there will be openings on specific dates. If you don't set a retirement-at-65 policy, you may have officers staying until they're 80."

But wasn't it hard for Harpole just to walk away after all he had been through with Pentair? "It's a policy I can live with," he said, his voice maintaining its matter-of-fact crispness. "It would be difficult to say, 'Do as I say, not as I do.'"

Merle N. Norman *(1887–1972)*

MERLE NORMAN COSMETICS

"If they like the results, they'll buy the products."

Few companies can match the perks that Merle Norman gives employees at its Sylmar, California, headquarters and plant. Anyone who works for the cosmetics maker can stop in at the employee cafeteria during lunch, and, for 25 cents, buy a seven-course meal featuring entrées like prime rib and trout amandine. Yvon Hunckler, the French chef who prepares this midday feast, also bakes the croissants, cakes, muffins, and cookies that are provided free to employees every morning and during coffee breaks.

If employees should develop cavities from eating these sweets, they can simply visit the company's staff dentist and have dental work done for about 10 percent of what it would normally cost. Other Merle Norman perks include: gas at wholesale prices from company-owned pumps; free first-run movies every other Saturday night at the company's lavish Cameo Theater; and a Christmas turkey luncheon buffet served up by the company's top executives, who also present each employee with a bonus check for an extra week's salary.

The Christmas buffet, and the company's overall benevolent attitude toward its employees, was inspired by Merle Nethercutt Norman, the woman who founded the firm in November 1931, just two months short of her 45th birthday.

A petite, energetic woman with burning dark eyes and black hair, Norman made it a policy to treat employees "like family" from her earliest days in business. Her empathy for the employees (mostly women) who performed the demanding task of mixing and packaging facial creams is easy to understand in light of her own earlier struggles to scratch out a living as a working woman.

Life was far from easy for Merle Norman before the success of her cosmetics company made her wealthy. She worked at a variety of menial jobs in the 1920s, never making enough money to afford more than the small bungalow she shared with her husband, parents, a niece, and two nephews.

Like most working women of her day, Merle Norman worked solely out of necessity. Her husband, Andy Norman, a tall, gregarious salesman who liked big cigars and racehorses, was never able to settle in one job long enough to be a consistent breadwinner. Married in 1913, the couple moved seven times during the next six years, crisscrossing the country from the Midwest to Arizona to the Deep South to New Jersey and back west again, as Andy vaguely pursued his dream of striking it rich—first in advertising, and then in real estate.

In 1919, the couple found themselves in Santa Monica, California, where Andy started a real estate business. After a promising start, the real estate agency began to falter, and, as he had done so often in the past, Andy began to talk of moving on in search of greener pastures.

This time, though, Merle Norman was not so ready to pick up stakes and take to the road. Hoping to establish deeper roots in Santa Monica, she persuaded her husband to back her in a small business of her own: a hamburger stand on the corner of Pier Avenue and Ocean Front. The stand quickly established itself as a popular lunch spot among the factory and warehouse workers in its neighborhood, thanks to its extra moist hamburger, the result of a secret recipe that called for mixing raw egg with chopped meat.

As popular as her hamburger stand was, though, Merle Norman soon realized that there was only a limited amount of money to be made operating a small restaurant that served only one product and had virtually all of its business concentrated during the lunch hour. In 1923, she closed her hamburger stand and moved into a new full-service restaurant that offered breakfast, lunch, and dinner.

Her new restaurant was undoubtably one of the shortest-lived business ventures ever recorded. In the company-published book *Merle Nethercutt Norman: An American Success Story,* Connie O'Kelley tells how Norman closed her restaurant early in its very first morning of existence, after an irate customer berated her for not having a waffle iron!

"The man stared at her, his heavy brows pulling into a deep frown. 'No waffle iron? And you call this a restaurant?'

"Merle's shoulders straightened and she abruptly placed her order pad in her apron pocket. 'No sir. . . . Not any more, I don't. You'll have to go somewhere else.'

"' . . . Somewhere else? What for?'

"'Because,' Merle said as she moved to open the door for him, 'we're closed.'

"' . . . But you just opened.'

"Merle's voice was grim. 'When you run a business, you're supposed to know your business. I didn't even know enough to get a waffle iron. So I'm closing.'"[1]

Closing the restaurant was a costly and humiliating experience for Norman, but it had not been in vain. She had learned a valuable lesson from it: the next time she started a business she would proceed more cautiously and plan more carefully. And, although she did not know it then, her next business would benefit from the advice and counsel of a particularly resourceful partner, her nephew Jack ("J. B.") Nethercutt.

J. B. Nethercutt came into his aunt's life in 1923, when he and his brother and sister were sent to live with Andy and Merle and Merle's parents following the death of their mother, Norman's sister, in Indiana. At the time, Merle had already closed the restaurant and was working as a lab assistant for Dr. Horace DuMoll, a small manufacturer of insecticides and cosmetics. Andy, meanwhile, was still struggling with his real estate business.

As a result of her DuMoll job, Norman began to experiment with her own cosmetics formulas. Returning from work in the evening, she would make different facial creams and skin lotions in her kitchen, using spare pots and pans and an old Roper stove.

By 1927, these experiments yielded a powder base ointment that Norman believed was good enough to sell to the public. But with the restaurant fiasco still very fresh in her memory, the 40-year-old entrepreneur did not want to plunge recklessly into this business. Keeping her job with DuMoll, Norman quietly began to sell her "Powder Cream" to friends and acquaintances.

Production of the product was still confined to the Norman kitchen, where Merle mixed batches of cream and her 12-year-old nephew, J. B., packaged it in small one-dollar jars. Gradually, Norman developed other beauty products, including "Miracol" skin lotion, "Cleansing Cream" cold cream, and a face powder that she sold in three-ounce bags for a dollar.

Unable to afford newspaper advertising, Norman relied on word-of-mouth referrals to attract new customers to her home studio. She encouraged these referrals by offering any customer who brought a friend to the studio a free makeover for herself and her guest.

Consisting of Cleansing Cream and Miracol treatments, followed by the application of powder base, rouge, powder, and lipstick, the makeovers were both costly and time-consuming. This led Andy Norman to warn his wife: "You'll work yourself to death with all those free demonstrations, not counting all the free material."

"Maybe so," Merle conceded. "But every free customer should mean a paying customer next time, because if they like the results, they'll buy the products."

History would prove Merle Norman correct. Promoting itself with the free makeover offer, her namesake firm grew into one of the most consistently profitable companies in the precarious cosmetics market. While the cosmetics empires of Arden and Rubinstein foundered in the 1970s and early 1980s, sales at the 2500 Merle Norman studios worldwide jumped from $60 million in 1978 to $180 million in 1983, aided by the company's continued policy of free product demonstrations.

These lofty figures are a far cry from the $9 a day that Merle Norman's first studio in Santa Monica was grossing in June 1932, when J. B. Nethercutt left college to join the business his aunt had started seven months earlier. A chemistry major at the California Institute of Technology, J. B. brought valuable technical skills to the new company. Working in the studio's small backroom laboratory, he developed a popular new Blush Rouge, as well as new varieties of Merle Norman lipstick, by the end of the summer.

"My background in chemistry made me very useful to my aunt's business," recalled Nethercutt, a distinguished silver-haired gentleman, who is the chairman, CEO, and sole owner of Merle Norman Cosmetics. "I ran much of the production end of the business for her, while she took care of sales and marketing. She needed someone with my particular skills, but I'm sure that if she didn't have me she would have found someone else and still succeeded. She was a very determined woman, and one who was very confident in her ultimate success."

Unable to have a child of her own following a 1914 miscarriage, Merle Norman regarded her nephew as a son. J. B. was one of her closest confidants, and she actively sought his advice on many matters, not just those involving the production of cosmetics.

On one occasion, J. B. acted as the mediator in a dispute between his aunt and uncle, and in the course of settling their argument, spawned a new marketing concept for the company. Seated in his plush California office in the spring of 1986, 72-year-old J. B. Nethercutt recounted the long-ago chain of events.

"We had a star saleswoman at our studio by the name of Blanche Martin, who was doing so well that my aunt got jealous and fired her. My uncle objected to this, because he didn't want to lose the sales that Blanche was writing up, and they got into an argument.

"I intervened and suggested, 'Why not let Blanche open a second Merle Norman studio in another city?' My aunt then said, 'It would have to be on the ends of the earth.' To which I replied, 'Well, would Santa Barbara be far enough?' That's how we came to open our second studio."

The Santa Barbara studio proved to be so successful that within a year of its 1934 opening there were seventy other Merle Norman studios. These were not franchised operations, but were independent businesses owned by operators who agreed to carry only Merle Norman products and adhere to other company standards.

By 1939, there were six hundred Merle Norman studios, located mainly in the West, South, and Midwest. The vast majority of these were owned by women, some of whom had scraped together their savings to open a studio after their husbands had been forced out of work during the Depression. In this respect, their situations closely paralleled that of the company founder herself.

At first, Merle Norman trained all new studio owners personally, but as her business grew, she had to devise other means of educating them. In 1936 she began publishing the *Merle Norman News* to keep dealers informed of new developments at the company. This was followed, two years later, by the Merle Norman Training School, which moved across the country providing ongoing sales training to studio owners.

The highlight of the company's studio owner training was its annual sales convention. Attracting studio owners from all over the country, the event provided an ideal showcase for what J. B. Nethercutt remembers as his aunt's greatest asset, her dynamic personality.

"My aunt Merle just overcame and overawed everyone in her presence," he said. "She was a wonderful public speaker who could captivate her audience in much the same way that Aimee Semple McPherson could. People were attracted by her dynamism, and she was very good at instilling enthusiasm in others. This ability served her very well when she was building the company."

Merle Norman first exhibited her magnetic personality as a girl in rural Cass County, Indiana. The oldest child of small-town grocer Melvin Nethercutt, Merle gained a measure of local fame at age 16, when she became the first girl to swim across the mile-and-a-half-wide Lake Maxinkuckee.

Defying her parents' wishes that she settle down after high school and marry a local boy, Merle went off to college in Chicago to earn a degree in teaching. After graduation, she became a teacher in South Bend, where she met and (against her parents' objections) married Andy Norman.

Years later, when Merle's small home cosmetics studio showed signs of developing into a real moneymaker, Andy closed his real estate office to become a partner in the business. Both of the Normans truly enjoyed the monetary rewards that their cosmetics firm bestowed upon them. They traveled frequently, owned a yacht, wore fine clothes, and lived in an impressive Mediterranean villa on Third Street in Santa Monica. Merle also found time to sponsor the Merle Norman Baseball League for Boys in Santa Monica and the Powder Puff Derby, a race for women aviators.

Merle Norman began to assume a less active role in the day-to-day affairs of her company following Andy's death in 1959. She officially retired four years later, withdrawing to "Rancho Merlita," a ranch she owned in Arizona—the state she and Andy had first moved to as newlyweds looking to strike it rich.

John Psarouthakis (1932–   )

J. P. INDUSTRIES

"Define a problem before trying to solve it."

John Psarouthakis was visiting Italy in late 1975 when he got into a serious car accident. Although it caused no permanent injuries, the crash did hospitalize the Greek-American businessman for three months, leaving him with plenty of time to think.

As Psarouthakis lay in bed, images from his first 43 years floated across his mind: his childhood on the island of Crete, where he had been orphaned at three and raised by two great-aunts . . . the four-line letter from America in 1951, "Congratulations. You have been accepted into the undergraduate program of the Massachusetts Institute of Technology" . . . the years in Boston, living at the home of an aunt, attending MIT by day and busing tables at the Ritz-Carlton by night . . . his Ph.D. in mechanical engineering from the University of Maryland . . . the rapid rise up the corporate ladder that led to the group vice-presidency of Masco Corporation, a diversified and very successful Detroit manufacturer.

Indeed, immigrant John Psarouthakis (pronounced Sa-roo-tá-kis) seemed to be the personification of the American Dream. His work at Masco in corporate development and acquisitions was exciting, his salary placed him in an upper-income bracket, and his family was loving and supportive.

Still, as he lay there mulling over the events of his life, the tall, craggy-faced executive became convinced that it was time for a change. "I enjoyed my work at Masco, and I liked and respected the Manoogians [company founder Alex Manoogian and his son, Richard], but the more I thought about my life, the stronger the desire to start my own business became," said Psarouthakis. "I wanted to have the freedom to try out my own ideas and implement my own plans and, if they worked out, to feel the satisfaction that comes from success and enjoy its financial rewards."

After he had recovered from his injuries, Psarouthakis took his Swedish-born wife, Inga, and their two sons, Michael and Peter, on a vacation to Crete and told them of his desire to strike out on his own. "They were behind me," he later recalled. "My wife and I drew up a two-year plan, budgeting what our living expenses would be and where the money would come from to meet them. Everyone agreed to make sacrifices while the business got off the ground; the boys gave up their allowances."

The Psarouthakis family's sacrifices were not in vain. The venture that John Psarouthakis founded, J. P. Industries, emerged as one of the hottest growth companies of the mid-1980s, its sales and net income jumping from $32 million and $1.1 million in fiscal 1982 to $234 million and $11 million in fiscal 1986. A public company since 1983 and a New York Stock Exchange company since 1986, J. P. Industries has seen the value of its stock soar by 240 percent since the company went public.

J. P. Industries has grown rich in a most unusual way for an American firm of the 1980s. It has not been involved in importing, retailing, or a service industry; and it has not developed a state-of-the-art high-technology product. Instead, the company plunged into two smokestack industries that had been all but given up for dead: plumbing supplies and transportation components (both original equipment manufacturer [OEM] and aftermarket).

Since 1979, Psarouthakis has bought out struggling manufacturers of prosiac products from sinks and toilets to camshafts and engine bearings and brought them back to life by reorganizing their production, management, and marketing operations.

Most acquisitions have responded quickly to his rescue efforts. DAB, a Troy, Michigan, manufacturer of engine bearings and transmission friction plates, was operating at a profit margin of less than 1.5 percent when J. P. Industries purchased it for $25 million in October 1985. One year later, this figure had increased to 8.5 percent.

Sitting in his comfortable office at J. P. Industries' Ann Arbor, Michigan, headquarters, Psarouthakis discussed the origins of his company. "I left Masco in 1978, after arranging for the smooth transition of my responsibilities there, and I started JPI on $500,000 seed capital. I provided some of the money myself (about $100,000), and the rest I raised from a small circle of friends and associates.

"My initial plan was the same as our plan today: to identify manufacturers of durable goods, except capital equipment, that were performing well below their potential, buy them at a good price (at about book value) turn them around, and integrate them into our corporation. Our intent was never simply to fix up an acquisition an then sell it; we were always interested in keeping companies for the long term."

The first step in restoring a sick company back to health, according to Psarouthakis, is to identify the problem or problems that caused its trouble. "One of the most valuable things I learned at MIT was to define a problem before trying to solve it," he said. "This not only applies to engineering and scientific research, but to any business endeavor, including the revitalization of a troubled company.

"Once we have defined at least the major problem that is making a company underperform, we can develop an action plan for solving it. After we do this, we will close the deal for the company and implement our plan to bring it back up to its potential."

By synergizing its acquisitions into a single corporate structure, J. P. Industries is able to improve the efficiency of each company, combining marketing and management functions, consolidating production, and eliminating overlapping products. After acquiring two faucet makers in the early 1980s, the company found itself with three factories producing 2200 different faucet models. JPI combined the two companies into a single, more profitable division with one management, one sales force, one factory, and a product line of 750 items.

Psarouthakis believes that companies most often become underperformers when management lacks leadership and direction, or when product lines are swollen with slow-moving items. Once they are identified, these problems can be solved, but other corporate maladies—such as a very negative image with customers—are usually incurable.

"I compare a troubled company to a sick person," said Psarouthakis. "Sometimes, the person who is sick can be nursed back to health, but other times the illness is terminal."

Psarouthakis has nursed more than a dozen ailing companies back to health. Some of them, like Briggs Plumbingware and McCord Gasket, are relatively well known. Others, like Precision Cold Forged Products of Plymouth, Michigan, are more obscure. All the rescued companies are involved in either the plumbing supply or transportation component industry.

Why did MIT-trained John Psarouthakis start a company in two rather mundane industries centered in the industrial Midwest, rather than embark on a more glamorous Silicon-Valley-type venture? Part of the answer lies in his earlier experience as a high-tech engineer developing power systems for spacecraft.

"For nine years I worked on energy conversion devices for the space program, first with a small company in Boston called Thermo Electron and then with the Martin Company [now Martin Marietta] in Baltimore," he recalled. "This experience educated me about the dangers involved in high-tech from a business standpoint.

"In a high-tech business, you are on the cutting edge of new developments, and thus your 'new product' can become obsolete before it's even introduced. It's very difficult to plan and project for a business in this situation. A developed market like housing or automobiles is relatively predictable. Thus, a person can make predictions about the number of housing starts or the number of new cars that will be built in the coming year and rarely be off by more than ten percent, which is no big deal. But in a high-tech business, one can make a prediction and be off by a hundred percent."

At the Martin Company, Psarouthakis headed a development laboratory that included twenty other scientists. This was his first real experience at managing a large number of people, and it was one that he would draw on later at J. P. Industries. "The development lab was a group of people working together to accomplish a common goal; in this respect, it was very similar to running a business. A lab manager, like a corporate executive, has to be a good motivator of people."

As he advanced at Martin, Psarouthakis found himself having to go to Washington more and more often to sell the company's projects to government officials. His impatience with the Washington bureaucracy, together with his increasing interest in management, led him to leave Martin in 1966 for a position in product planning and development with Allis-Chalmers Corporation, a firm more oriented toward the private sector.

Psarouthakis remained with the agricultural and electrical equipment maker for four years, continuing his career movement away from research and toward management. Then, in 1970, an event occurred that had a profound impact on his life: he was hired as vice-president of planning and engineering at Masco Corporation.

Founded back in 1929 by Armenian immigrant Alex Manoogian, Masco was a profitable medium-sized company best known for its single-handled "Delta" faucet. Then, in 1968, the founder's son, Richard Manoogian, joined the firm and embarked on a very successful diversification program, acquiring dozens of companies making unglamorous products like luggage racks, wheel spindles, and oil drilling heads. Largely as a result of this diversification, Masco's sales increased from $69.4 million in 1970 to over $726.4 million in 1979.

Masco provided Psarouthakis with an obvious role model for J. P. Industries. But the Greek-born entrepreneur drew more than inspiration from his former employer; he also acquired a great deal of experience at Masco that would later help him at his own firm.

As one of the four top officers at Masco, Psarouthakis was actively involved in the company's rapid diversification, and indeed, he made many valuable contributions to its success. He created Masco's first five-year corporate plan, he oversaw the opening of its European operations, and he supervised efforts to turn around troubled acquisitions.

Unlike Masco, however, which had the capital needed to acquire profitable companies, J. P. Industries had limited resources when it started and could only afford to buy companies that were losing money or, at best, breaking even. The company's first acquisition, purchased with financing from the National Bank of

Detroit, was American Metalcraft, a $2.8 million Waterville, Ohio, specialty stamping company. Although struggling to stay in the black at the time of the acquisition, American Metalcraft quickly developed into a very profitable business under its new owner and is still an important part of J. P. Industries today.

Psarouthakis was not so fortunate with his second acquisition, Fabric Filters Corporation, a maker of a self-cleaning dust filter. He planned to mass-produce the filter, but it could not be turned out efficiently in high volume. In the end, he decided to shut down the filter plant and license the manufacturing process to others.

"This was our worst setback at JPI, but fortunately it wasn't bad and it happened early in our history," said Psarouthakis. "You have to be prepared to accept and handle failure when you take risks; otherwise, it can have a catastrophic effect on your career. If you know how to handle failure, you can bounce back from it and try again."

Psarouthakis "bounced back" from his mild reversal with a vengeance, piling successful acquisition on top of successful acquisition, until he had established a thriving mini-conglomerate with plants in the U.S., Germany, and England.

A gracious, scholarly man who speaks with a distinctive Greek accent, Psarouthakis offered this perspective on his own mid-life success. "I probably was much more thorough in planning things out at 45 than I would have been at 25. After all, I had more to lose; I was getting paid very well at Masco. But regardless of how thorough you are, there is a point at which you must take action. You can't analyze and plan forever."

Anthony T. Rossi (1900–   )

TROPICANA JUICE

"Control—that is the most important thing...."

One can easily imagine how the top brass at Kellogg must have felt on that August day in 1977 when they learned that the proposed merger between the nation's largest breakfast cereal maker and Tropicana, the leading purveyor of orange juice, had fallen through for the third time in as many years.

On the surface, at least, the Kellogg-Tropicana marriage seemed like a match made in heaven. Both companies were strongly associated with a popular breakfast staple. Both had long been among the profit leaders in the food industry. And Kellogg's buyout offer of $382 million was considered generous by most of the directors on the Tropicana board.

But just as its two previous offers had been, Kellogg's third proposal was spurned at the altar by Tropicana's tough septuagenarian founder, chairman, and undisputed leader, Anthony Rossi. Only a month away from his seventy-seventh birthday, Rossi was obviously well past retirement age. Although he was generally in good health, he knew that there would soon come a day when he would no longer be able to run a large multinational corporation. Having no children to hand over the reins of power to, he seriously considered the offers of corporate suitors like Kellogg. But when it came time to finalize a merger agreement, the Italian immigrant still could not bring himself to let

173

go of the business he had started thirty years earlier as a small, backroom packing operation.

Even by the most romantic entrepreneurial standards, Rossi's devotion to Tropicana was intense. The deeply tanned, craggy-faced businessman actively involved himself in every facet of the company he called "my baby"—whether it meant fixing a faulty bottling machine, helping a factory worker iron out a personal problem, or taste-testing each day's output of orange juice.

"I am the quality control," he once declared in his still thick Italian accent. "I just happen to have very keen taste. If I taste oil too much, they put the juice in the oil centrifuge. Too much air—it goes through the de-aerator."[1]

Looking back on his career, the orange juice millionaire offered this explanation for his success: "Control—that is the most important thing in business. You must have control, so you can correct anything that is going wrong."[2]

True to his word, Anthony Rossi built Tropicana into a vertically integrated company that controlled virtually every facet of its orange juice operation. Oranges were extracted and their juice processed by equipment custom designed by Rossi and built in the company's own steel-fabricating plant. Juice was packaged in bottles made in the company's glass plant or in cartons from its carton plant. Then the finished product was shipped in company trucks, company railroad cars, or even in a company steamship.

In 1957, the juice maker launched the 8000-ton S. S. Tropicana, the first ocean-going vessel designed to transport orange juice. Every eight days the ship would be loaded with a million gallons of frozen orange slush at Cape Canaveral, Florida, for a trip to the Tropicana bottling plant in Queens, New York. By the time the journey was completed, the slush had gained about 2.5 degrees in temperature, enough to turn it into chilled, ready-to-be-bottled juice.

"The orange juice tanker was just one example of Tony's creativity," recalled Ed Price, a former Tropicana vice-president and a longtime associate of Rossi's. "The man was a genius in many ways, particularly in matters that involved engineering. Tropicana developed a great many patented innovations over the years, and most of them came out of Tony's imagination."

Indeed, there are many in the Florida citrus industry who say

22. Anthony Rossi welcomes the S.S. Tropicana as she steams up the East River to the Whitestone, Queens, orange juice plant, circa 1958. The first and only ocean tanker used to transport orange juice, it was taken out of service 169 voyages later on June 4, 1961.

that it was Rossi's imagination that was responsible for creating the chilled-juice industry in the years following World War II.

A small Bradenton, Florida, packer who sold chilled citrus sections to restaurants, Rossi was looking for something to do with oranges that were too small or too spotted to be included in his fruit cups when he came up with the idea of extracting their juice and selling it in gallon jugs.

At first Rossi limited the distribution of his juice to nearby hotels and restaurants because of its tendency to spoil quickly, even when refrigerated. Then, in the early 1950s, he patented an aseptic vacuum packing method that greatly preserved the juice's freshness. With the shelf life of his product extended, the Florida entrepreneur was able to start bottling orange juice in volume and distributing it over a wide area. He built a high-speed processing plant in Bradenton and acquired a fleet of refrigerated trucks to deliver juice to big city dairies in the North. (Dairies were selected as the first distributors of Tropicana because of their experience in handling milk and other perishable food products.)

Tony Rossi's success with Tropicana marked the first time that citrus juice was bottled and sold on a large commercial scale. Prior to the introduction of Tropicana, people from outside the citrus belt who wanted orange juice had to squeeze it from the fruit themselves.

The only other alternative was frozen concentrated orange juice, which was just being introduced at about this time. In fact, Rossi invested $30,000 in one of the earliest juice concentrators in 1949, but he dropped out of the concentrate market five years later—not to return for two decades—to devote his full attention to chilled juice.

Finding new ways to increase the efficiency of chilled-juice production became almost an obsession for Rossi. Putting in 60- and 70-hour weeks at his Bradenton plant, the immigrant juice maker pioneered a series of major processing and packaging innovations. He invented one of the first high-speed glass decorating machines to label Tropicana bottles; he was the first to package juice in dairy-style cartons; and he was the first to market citrus juice in vending machines.

But Rossi's most significant innovation was the flash pasteurizer, a device that forced juice through a series of small tubes at high speeds and sent its temperature roller-coasting from 32 degrees to 180 degrees and back down to 32 degrees, all within three seconds. The new pasteurization method opened a new world of marketing opportunities for Tropicana by making it possible to ship and store orange juice without refrigeration.

With Tropicana's umbilical cord to the refrigerated display case cut, Rossi was able to distribute juice to a much wider variety of retail outlets. He proceeded to expand the company's market steadily throughout the 1960s, and by the end of the decade Tropicana juice was being sold in every state and twenty foreign countries.

Tropicana's large international market required a reliable

year-round orange juice pipeline, one that was not dependent on the season cycles of citrus farming. Rossi ensured that his bottling plant would have an uninterrupted supply of product by freezing 20-lb. slabs of juice during the peak growing months when oranges were plentiful, and then thawing them for bottling during the off-season.

The infamous 1962 frost that devastated Florida's citrus crop provided the Tropicana founder with another springboard for his fertile imagination. With his local supply of oranges cut off, Rossi quickly assembled an extraction plant on a ship and steamed to a point off the Mexican coast, where he began processing that nation's abundant and cheap orange crop. This plan had to be abandoned a short time later, however, after the Mexican government accused Tropicana of piracy and drove the ship away.

Tony Rossi's genius as a production and packaging engineer belies his lack of formal education. Born at the turn of the century in Messina, Sicily, Rossi was an undistinguished pupil at the local secondary school before he joined the Grenadier Guards at 17.

After leaving the military in 1921, the 21-year-old Italian journeyed to America, where he hoped to earn enough money to finance an adventure film that he and four friends planned to make about the Belgian Congo. Rossi settled in New York and toiled at a variety of jobs, including cab driver, bricklayer, chauffeur, and heavyweight boxer—he was six-foot-four and weighed 240 lbs.—before opening a small grocery in Jackson Heights, Queens, in 1928.

By this time, Rossi had forgotten all about returning home to make the African film. "Tony took very well to this country," said Ed Price. "He was determined early on to live out the American Dream—and he certainly did just that."

The Queens grocery, one of the earliest self-service food stores in New York, gave Tony Rossi's Horatio Alger dream its first real shape and direction. After seven years of hopscotching from one menial job to the next, Rossi was now in the food industry, an industry he would remain active in for the next half century.

At his grocery, Rossi developed many of the merchandising ideas that would later be used to build the Tropicana empire.

The grocery's specialty was "one-day-old eggs," a commodity that Rossi drove out to the countryside each night to buy. Rossi would later recall how he had no trouble selling his eggs at a premium price, "because people will gladly pay more for freshness." Years later, he applied this principle to Tropicana, eschewing frozen concentrate in favor of chilled orange juice, which, despite its higher price, claimed a large consumer following because it was closer in taste to fresh-squeezed juice.

As a grocer, Rossi also gained insights into the workings of dairy distribution. He saw that dairies were skilled at handling perishable products that required constant refrigeration from warehouse to delivery truck to store display. He saw, too, that most dairies were eager to complement their milk, butter, and ice cream lines with other perishable foods to help defray the high cost of refrigerated distribution. Thus, when the former grocer began mass-producing chilled juice, he knew that he would find plenty of willing distributors among the nation's dairies.

Would Tony Rossi have been aware that such a strong network of experienced distributors lay waiting for his new product had he not been a grocer? The question, of course, is impossible to answer. But it is safe to assume that he would have at least been slower to recognize this built-in solution to his distribution needs had he not had experience dealing with dairies as a store owner.

After running his grocery for 13 years, Rossi, who never liked New York winters, moved south to Virginia in 1941 to farm tomatoes. One year later, he moved again; this time to Bradenton, where he rented a small tomato farm and opened a cafeteria.

The cafeteria proved to be much more successful than the farm, so Rossi soon opened a second location in Miami Beach— "the biggest restaurant on the beach." Then, wartime gas rationing and a temporary ban on dog and horse racing cut deeply into the city's tourist trade, and the newly arrived restaurateur found himself staring at a room full of empty tables.

Rossi sold his Miami Beach restaurant in 1945 and retreated to Bradenton, where he started a small business selling citrus fruit gift baskets to Macy's, Gimbel's, and other northern department stores. Two years later, the 47-year-old entrepreneur bought a bankrupt grapefruit packing plant for $15,000 and started Fruit Industries, Inc., to market chilled citrus sections to restaurants.

23. The Tropicana girl colophon helped Anthony Rossi create a readily identifiable image for his new product in the 1950s. The "original" Tropic-Anna was Anna Kesten, the daughter of Rossi's purchasing agent, who served as the model for the trademark illustration.

In 1955, Rossi renamed his company Tropic-Anna, a name that he had been using for several years on his popular line of chilled citrus juices. The original "Tropic-Anna" was Anna Kesten, the young daughter of Rossi's purchasing agent.

After having thrice rejected Kellogg's merger offers, Rossi finally acknowledged the toll of the years and sold Tropicana to Beatrice Foods for a reported $495 million in 1978.[3] He remained on the Tropicana board for a time after the sale, before leaving to concentrate on running the Aurora Foundation, an organization he established to provide elderly Christian missionaries with free retirement housing.

Although he was born Catholic, Rossi became a devout Baptist in his thirties. For years, he served as a church deacon and Sunday school teacher in Bradenton. He also built one of the first Baptist churches in Italy and, on occasion, went to his hometown of Messina to preach on the street corners. Not surprisingly, the deeply religious businessman downplayed the importance of his personal wealth. "There is no real happiness to be found in gathering material things," he once preached. "The more you get, the more you want. What real inner happiness is there in having cars, boats, furs—such items as that?"

Nevertheless, as the owner of two homes and a large saltwater swimming pool, Rossi hardly lived a life of monasterial austerity. But, in fairness, it should be noted that the citrus millionaire did put most of the huge fortune he had amassed from the sale of Tropicana into a trust fund for the Aurora Foundation and other charitable organizations. "Tony felt the Lord had been good to him, and he wanted to share his good fortune with others," said Ed Price. "He gave away millions and never sought publicity as a philanthropist."

Although no longer involved in Tropicana, Tony Rossi is still, at 85, taking an active role in running the Aurora Foundation. The orange juice pioneer is convinced that the hand of God has played a big role in molding the shape of his successful career. "Without God I wouldn't have anything. He has given me everything."

Still, the Tropicana founder always subscribed to the view that "the Lord helps those who help themselves." Asked what an entrepreneur needs to succeed after 40, he quickly rattled off a list: "ambition, persistence, creativity, and common sense." Four qualities he had obviously been blessed with to an extraordinary degree.

24. *Isbell's Rush Street restaurant in Chicago was a popular dining spot with local residents and out-of-town visitors. The restaurant featured live entertainment and was the scene of many parties for the city's rich and famous.*

VII

Building
a Nest

Tom Duck (1913–   )

UGLY DUCKLING RENT-A-CAR SYSTEM, INC.

"Some people just take a little bit longer than others to get there."

In 1977, a 63-year-old former insurance salesman named Tom Duck used $10,000 of his savings to start what he thought would be an entertaining retirement project. He took the money to a used car lot, where it bought him nine clean automobiles in good running condition. Adding a tenth vehicle of his own, Duck lined up the fleet in front of his rural home near Tucson, Arizona, and, with his wife Junia, started a business renting used cars at rates much lower than those of Hertz or Avis.

"We started out at $4.95 a day and a nickel a mile at a time when the big guys were getting $15, $20, and even $25 a day," Duck recalled. "The difference, of course, was that their cars were new and ours were used. But I figured that people wouldn't mind renting safe, dependable used cars if they could save some money.

"The whole thing just struck me as a good idea that nobody ever tried before. We had a lot of used cars of our own sitting around our twelve-acre property, and they'd always been good transportation for us. So one day I thought, if we rented cars just like the ones we're driving, what's wrong with that?"

The American public, it turned out, agreed that there was nothing wrong with Duck's idea at all. Not only did his low rates strike a responsive chord with budget-minded motorists, but his concept of renting previously owned automobiles attracted en-trepreneurs in search of an innovative business opportunity.

185

25. Tom Duck, who started the nation's fifth largest car rental agency as a "retirement project," did not have to look too far for a name for his new business: he called it Ugly Duckling.

Within months after renting his first vehicle, Duck was getting inquiries from people who wanted to know how they could set up a similar operation in Albuquerque or Des Moines or Peoria, and—just like that—Duck was in the franchise business. Less than a decade after it started, his front-yard enterprise had become the nation's fifth largest car rental chain, with nearly 600 franchised outlets in all but a handful of states.

One of the most impressive things about Ugly Duckling Rent-A-Car System, Inc., is the speed with which it has grown. "It took Ray Kroc five years to get his two hundredth franchise going. In five years we had *three* hundred franchises. So you can say that we're running ahead of McDonald's," the company founder pointed out.

Duck attributes this rapid expansion to the fact that Ugly Duckling has identified and targeted a specific niche in the car rental market, a niche that the larger companies, with their emphasis on the business traveler, have overlooked. "Our typical customer is not the corporate executive on an expense account, but the average American who is paying for the rental out of his or her pocket and wants something cheap. It might be someone who's own car is in service, or a family who's vacationing in another city.

"Because we're not aiming at the business traveler, we don't have to be in expensive airport locations, and this helps us cut costs further and offer even lower rates. We're in a lot of small towns, some with populations of only a couple thousand. Middle America is our forte—and women. Forty percent of our customers are women—four times the industry average. They don't have plastic cards to charge off cars to corporations."

None of these demographic concerns, however, were on Tom Duck's mind back in February 1977, when he bought his first nine cars, among which were a Chevy, a Toyota, and an AMC Gremlin. "If you'd have told me this would be anything but an interesting hobby for Mrs. D. and me, I'd never have believed it. We just wanted to start a retirement project that would bring in a little extra money," he insisted.

Duck first realized he was "on to something" at the end of his first year in business. Earlier, the local Tucson NBC affiliate had been out to do a story on the Ducks and their no-frills rental cars. The feature aired on the five o'clock news, and immediately afterward phone calls started coming from prospective customers.

"The TV thing carried us for months," Duck said. "People would tell other people about us, and we soon had to move to a commercial site in town. From there, we grew even faster."

The business was helped by its location in a popular tourist state. Many of Duck's early clients were vacationers who wanted a vehicle for touring the scenic highways of Arizona and the Southwest. His very first rental was to a couple who drove round-trip to Albuquerque, New Mexico. They were charged a fee of more than $300, but realized that this was a substantial savings over what they would have spent with a national car rental company.

When out-of-state customers returned home, they often told friends and relatives about the "deal" they had gotten on a rental car. This, said Duck, was how the first Ugly Duckling franchises got started. "We'd get a call from someone in a place like Kansas or Iowa who'd say, 'My brother rented a car from you, and I was wondering how I could start a business like yours. I think it's a great idea.'"

By the end of 1977, the Ducks had sold seven franchises, all unsolicited. A year later, on January 1, 1979, they formed Ugly Duckling Rent-A-Car System, Inc. (a separate company from their rental agency), to sell and license franchises.

At first, most new franchisees continued to be drawn into the Ugly Duckling fold through word of mouth. Tom and Junia Duck did very little active promotion of their used-car rental agency concept, with the exception of running a small ad in *Automotive Age*. But as the business grew, it became apparent that a more aggressive selling effort was needed. So the Ducks, now joined by their son, Tom, Jr., put together a national sales organization made up largely of individuals who already owned Ugly Duckling franchises.

"We like to use our own people as salesmen," Duck explained, "because they can give prospective franchisees a realistic picture of what to expect; they're not going to promise the moon. And they're certainly not going to encourage someone who would be a detriment to their investment to join the chain."

Each new franchisee pays a one-time, up-front fee of $3500. Once the agency is in operation, the franchisee pays the parent company royalties of six percent on all time-mileage revenues taken in on a monthly basis.

By 1984, there were more than 500 franchised Ugly Duckling outlets doing a combined annual volume of $49.7 million, bringing Tom Duck considerable personal wealth at a stage in his life that he had, at one time, expected to spend in comfortable, but modest, retirement.

Not surprisingly, the trim, tennis-playing septuagenarian told an interviewer, "If I had a miracle wand, I wouldn't want to turn my life back to 40.

"I might have blown it or failed to sense the idea earlier in life," he added. "I had been gaining seasoning all along the way. ... I'd like to think I was preparing myself for what eventually happened. Some people just take a little bit longer than others to get there."

As a young man with a degree in business administration from the University of Arizona, the Ugly Duckling founder took a considerable amount of time to settle into any occupation. His pre-40 career was marked by frequent switches from vocation to vocation, including several short-lived attempts at operating businesses of his own.

After graduating from college, Duck opened a gas station in Tucson and later became a construction worker. Following his marriage, he entered the retailing field, working first for Montgomery Ward and then as a manager-trainee at Sears. Frustrated by his slow progress through the department store hierarchy, he left Sears after a few years to open his own appliance store in Indianapolis, which he operated until World War II.

Duck spent the war years as a naval deck officer stationed in the Pacific. In 1946, following his release from the Navy, he and his family settled in southern California, where he decided to make a new start in the toy manufacturing business. Why toys? "Because I had some ideas and thought it would be fun," he explained.

Two of Duck's ideas, a toy chest shaped like a drum and a textured paint-by-number set, were modest successes in the retail marketplace. But their designer eventually grew bored with the day-to-day routine of running a factory, and, in the early 1950s, sold his company. Next, Duck tried distributing a line of dishwashers and garbage disposals for a California manufacturer. When that left him uninspired, he decided it was time to fall back on a profession for which he had received some training in college—selling insurance. ("I was pushing 40, and I didn't want to see myself hedgehopping all my life.")

Insurance proved to be the career niche that had heretofore eluded Duck. He stayed in the profession for nearly twenty-five years, earning the title of Chartered Life Underwriter and winning numerous sales awards and contests. He became the first at his agency to sell a million dollars worth of life insurance in one month.

Duck later recounted how he had motivated himself as a salesman: "I never worked to become wealthy per se; I'd work for prizes, trips, and possessions. If I wanted a Lincoln Continental, I'd make enough money to go out and buy it. I'd just look at the guy in the mirror every morning and say, 'Hey, if you want this or that, go out and make the money.'"

Duck's self-administered pep talks brought him the trimmings of the California Good Life, including the first built-in swimming pool in his Ontario subdivision. But by the mid-1970s the hustle and the L.A. smog had gotten to him, and he and Junia, their children grown, moved to Tucson and retirement.

The surprising turn of fortune that his life has taken since then is one Tom Duck seems to have fully adjusted to. Like one of Murphy's laws, his expectations for Ugly Duckling Rent-A-Car System, Inc., have expanded along with the size of the chain.

At 73, his long-range goals for the company are, first, to cover more cities than industry leader Hertz, and, second, to have six thousand Ugly Duckling locations across the U.S. "I'm not thinking small," he declared.

Nor is Duck particularly concerned about the rash of competitors that have entered the used-car rental market in recent years. "They rent junk," he scoffed. "We do not want to be mentioned in the same breath as those people. Our cars are decent, reliable transportation."

Finding a steady supply of suitable used vehicles has not been a problem for Ugly Duckling, since most of the company's franchise operators are automobile dealers who get their rental cars from the trade-ins they take in. This arrangement was by design, and it has worked to the benefit of both dealers and rental customers, said Duck, explaining, "Certain used models have a low resale value, but are very desirable as rental cars. In the early '80s when gas prices were high, the Chrysler New Yorker wasn't the hottest thing on the used car lot, but renters were delighted to have its deluxe features—cruise control, power windows, and so forth."

Before a used car is admitted into Ugly Duckling's fleet, it must undergo a safety inspection. The inspections, as well as all service work on rental cars, are performed by K mart Auto Service Centers. Duck has entered into a fleet care contract with K mart, under which the auto centers keep computerized service and maintenance records on all Ugly Duckling vehicles.

As far as Tom Duck is concerned, the appearance of a vehicle's exterior and upholstery is almost as important as its condition underneath the hood. "We stress cleanliness inside and out, because such a large percentage of our customers are women—and women don't want to get into a dirty-looking car.

"Another thing women like about us," he added, "is our little duck logo. It's on all of our key chains, and it evokes a lot of comment."

Duck, who has always recognized the public relations value of his name, originally had the smiling cartoon duck designed for his toy company. Once he decided to recycle it as a logo for his car rental agency, the name "Ugly Duckling" suggested itself—one of the many things about the business that just seemed to fall in place.

But the company founder insists that most people fail to grasp the full meaning behind the "ugly duckling" concept. "I looked up 'ugly duckling' in the dictionary, and the definition is, 'An unpromising child that turns out later to have exceptional intelligence or beauty.' But most people just take it to mean a person or thing that's ugly—period. The part they don't realize," he said, pausing perhaps to reflect on the parallel in his own business career, "is that there is a happy ending."

Marion W. Isbell (1905-)

RAMADA INNS

"All of my life I tried to get ahead by outworking the guy next to me."

Marion Isbell was attending a Chicago banquet in 1940, when he was asked to say a few words about his remarkable rise from poor orphan to millionaire restaurateur. A tall, very thin man who looked as if he could have been the supporting star in a matinee Western, Isbell began by recounting the story of his childhood in Whitehaven, Tennessee.

"When I was in school, I could see very clearly that so many of the kids were much smarter than I was. I don't know whether this was because of my poor nutrition or something else, but reading and remembering were extremely hard for me. I just didn't seem to catch on as quickly as the other youngsters.

"Then, when I moved to Chicago at 16, I figured that I might at least be smarter than these dumb Yankees," he continued. "But I soon learned that the folks in Chicago were not so dumb. It hit me that I would never be able to outsmart anyone, so I decided to outwork them. This, I soon realized, was not too difficult to do."

All of those at the gathering laughed off Isbell's self-deprecating remarks about his intellectual shortcomings, but no one doubted his claims about hard work. In his 35 years, Isbell had sweated through enough hours of grueling manual labor to last a couple of lifetimes. At 8, he was picking cotton from half-past three until dark on school days and dawn to dusk on Saturdays.

During the summer he worked the cotton fields twelve hours a day, with an hour off for lunch, six days a week.

"Anyone who has picked cotton is highly motivated to find a better way of life," Isbell would later recall in a voice that sounds remarkably like Walter Brennan's. "For an 8-year-old kid with a sack and a strap hung round your neck, it begins to hurt pretty bad. You're bending down all the time, walking on your knees, and of course the cotton has stick in it. Reaching in for the cotton was pretty torturous; my hands would be bleeding."

Things got only a little easier for Isbell after he moved north as a teenager. Arriving in Chicago, he found a job as a busboy, working twelve hours a day, seven days a week, for $10 plus free meals. Then he became ill and was fired. After his recovery, he became a dishwasher and was making $14 a week, working six ten-hour days. At the time he thought that this job was "heaven."

Eventually, Isbell's hard work began to pay off. In 1928, six years after arriving in Chicago almost penniless, he was making $55 a week operating a leased soda fountain at Portes Drug Store in Evanston. He then went on to lease fountains at other drug stores, hiring soda jerks to manage them for a salary of $40 a week plus 50 percent of the profits. By 1934 he had fifteen leased soda fountains that were netting him an annual income of $20,000.

Undeterred by America's lingering depression, Isbell continued to amass his fortune. In 1935 he started Isbell's, a chain of middle- to upper-level restaurant/cocktail lounges featuring live entertainment. By the middle of the next decade, he owned ten prosperous restaurants. In recognition of his skills, Isbell was elected president of the National Restaurant Association. During World War II, he was appointed chief administrator of the Office of Price Administration's institutional-user rationing branch.

But Isbell's back-breaking work pace was not without its costs. A three-pack-a-day cigarette smoker, he developed serious respiratory problems while still in his thirties. Under his doctor's orders, he began to scale down his business activities in 1946, selling his Chicago restaurants and retiring to a warmer climate in Tucson, where he planned to raise orchids.

The work ethic had become too deeply ingrained in Isbell, however, to allow him to retire quietly. In 1950, he returned to Chicago and the restaurant business. Later, he was selected by the Atomic Energy Commission to develop food preparation techniques that could be used to feed survivors of a nuclear war.

"We took the tops off 10- and 20-pound lard cans, hung chunks of meat inside, layered vegetables on the bottom, replaced the lids, and suspended the cans over open fires," he recalled, describing one of his experiments.

By 1955, Isbell was back in Arizona, where he joined four investors who had recently started to build small motels along the new limited-access highways. Less than a year later, the group added another member, Del Webb, the co-owner of the New York Yankees. These investors controlled 19 motels, primarily in the Southwest, by the end of 1958.

"This was a very loosely organized business," recalled Isbell. "Our motels went by all sorts of different names; some were the Flamingo, others were the Hi Way House, the Baghdad, or the Sahara. The motels had no common architectural style, no common signage, and no common advertising. Each one was more or less a business unto itself."

Isbell's own experience with his soda fountains and restaurants had taught him the value of running a multiple-location business as a single chain. "You have a much easier time creating a strong public image with a chain; plus, it's much more efficient from a management standpoint. I knew this from Chicago, but I had a hard time impressing the point on some of my associates."

Eventually, Isbell was able to convince the other investors to group their collection of motels into a single, identifiable chain. In 1959, they began calling all their locations Ramada Inns, a name taken from the Spanish term for "shady resting place." Two years later, the company was incorporated as Ramada Inns, Inc., with Marion Isbell as president.

At the time of its incorporation, Ramada had 25 company-owned and franchised inns. This number grew to 100 in 1965, when the company went international by opening a hotel in Morocco, and over 260 in 1969, when Ramada was listed on the New York Stock Exchange.

The Ramada marketing plan under Isbell was simple: to offer clean and comfortable rooms at affordable prices, with ample free parking, easy check-in, and a location right off the highway. It was a strategy virtually identical to the one followed by Ra-

26. Marion Isbell at the downtown Phoenix Ramada Inn circa 1960. The motel opened in 1956 as the "Sahara," one of many names used by the company until Isbell created a uniform chainwide image built around the Ramada Inn trademark.

mada's chief rival and motel industry leader, Holiday Inn, which was itself founded by a middle-aged businessman, 39-year-old Charles Kemmons Wilson, in 1952.

"Our plan was to compete with Holiday by offering rooms that were as good or better than theirs at a substantially lower rate," said Isbell. "I don't think we ever hurt Holiday any, but we did OK for ourselves. There was plenty of room for both of us at the time; people were taking to the new interstates just as fast as the government was building them, and they all needed places to stay when they traveled."

Former restaurateur Isbell did manage to distinguish Ramada from its rivals, including Holiday, by departing from the industry tradition of having low-keyed restaurants accessible only from the lobby and intended primarily for guests. Ramada was one of the first motel chains to draw attention to its restaurants by giving them their own distinct name ("Chez Bon"), separate outside entrances, prominent signage, and thematic decors and menus.

Ramada's high-profile restaurants, which succeeded in attracting local diners as well as motel guests, were a major contributor to the company's success. In 1968, food and beverage sales accounted for $16.2 million of the company's $59.7 million total volume.

As a restaurateur, Marion Isbell developed an appreciation for advertising: he spent $5000 on the first full-color restaurant ad in the *Chicago Tribune* to promote a $2.05 chateaubriand dinner special. Isbell carried this attitude over to Ramada, where he collected as much as 8¢ per room per day from franchisees to finance an advertising campaign that included billboards, TV (*The Dating Game* and *The Johnny Cash Show*), magazines (*Mademoiselle*), and cooperative agreements with oil companies and car rental agencies.

Like Holiday Inn with its multicolored sparkler sign, and Howard Johnson's with its bright orange roof, Isbell wanted Ramada to have a trademark that would be readily identifiable to highway travelers. Early in its history, the chain developed its Ramada coachman sign and its slogan, "Luxury for Less."

By the time Isbell retired to a hilltop mansion overlooking Paradise Valley, Arizona, in 1973, the red-and-white Ramada sign appeared on close to 700 inns throughout the world. Years later, as he approached his eighty-first birthday, the orphan from Tennessee discussed his career.

"People have asked me to tell them the secret to my success. Well, there is no secret. I was fortunate to find a good opportunity with Ramada, and the rest was just plain old hard work.

"All of my life I tried to get ahead by outworking the guy next to me. This didn't always make me very popular: one time in Chicago a group of fellows threatened to throw me out the window because I was washing dishes too fast and making them look bad in front of the restaurant owner. But you can't worry

27. The first Ramada Inn opened in Flagstaff, Arizona, as the "Flamingo" in 1954. The motel's sign and the design of its main building drew attention to its restaurant, a feature that former restaurateur Isbell used to make his locations stand out from the competition.

about what other people think when you want to get ahead. You just got to put your head down and work as hard as you can."

Isbell concedes that his hard-work philosophy is not for everyone. "I guess it all depends on what you want out of life. You certainly can't teach anybody how to work hard. You can't learn it from books, and you can't learn it in school. It's something that's got to be burning inside of you."

Marion Isbell's burning work drive was ignited by the dire poverty of his youth. The second of three children, Isbell was not yet five when he and his brothers—James, seven, and Leon, three—were placed in a Memphis orphanage in 1910 following the death of their mother. The boys' father, a struggling farmer, was killed in a plowing accident six months later, leaving an insurance policy that paid the orphanage $15 a month for their care.

"The orphanage didn't have enough money to feed us properly," recalled Isbell. "There were a lot of hungry days. If you had beans to eat, you had beans. If you had potatoes, you had only potatoes."

197

In 1913, the boys returned to the small family farm to live with an aunt who had just left her husband. Isbell would remember these times as being even more unbearable than the three years spent at the orphanage. "Things were unbelievably rough. For a while we continued to get the $15 a month, but that was about all we had. We ate mostly black-eyed peas, potatoes, and a few things my aunt canned from the garden. I rarely got enough to eat. My aunt would dish up our plate, and that was all we got; if you were still hungry, too bad."

Isbell and his brother James went to Chicago seeking a better future in 1922, but like their ill-fitting clothes and Tennessee accents, poverty seemed to follow them north. Their low point occurred when the cafeteria where they were employed closed, leaving both of them out of work.

Unable to find work for weeks, the brothers saw their meager savings vanish. "We got down to where, between us, my brother and I had two dimes left. We were behind in our room rent, but the landlady knew we were trying and went along with us. We used the twenty cents to buy a can of beans and a loaf of bread, which we ate for dinner."

Luckily, Marion and James found jobs as dishwashers the next day. From dishwashing, Marion advanced to working drug store soda fountains. Then came the business leasing fountains from pharmacists.

"The drug store owners weren't interested in their soda fountains," he said. "This wasn't their primary business. They more or less had the fountains in their stores because customers expected to find a soda fountain in a drug store. Very few drug stores made real money on their fountains, so it was fairly easy to talk storeowners into leasing their fountains to me. I knew that I could do well at this because I was in the soda fountain business, not the drug store business."

Although his leased soda fountains made money, Marion Isbell never envisioned becoming a millionaire. "It didn't occur to me until I owned a few restaurants. Before that, I just took things one day at a time.

"I was scared and broke all of my life until I was 20," he continued. "At first all I wanted to do was climb out of poverty. When I was making $10 a week as a dishwasher, my big goal was to make

$20 or $25, so I could buy a used automobile and maybe take a girl out on a date."

Isbell eventually dated, and in 1927 he married a girl named Ingrid Helsing, whose family was in the restaurant business. A year later, Ingrid quit her job at Lerner's Dress Shop to help Isbell operate the soda fountains he was beginning to lease. Her brother, William Helsing, would become Isbell's partner in the Isbell's Restaurant chain and an early investor in Ramada Inns.

Looking back on his two business achievements, Isbell compared pre- and post-40 success. "For me it was easier after 40, because I was already well off and I had a lot of experience, a good credit rating, and a good reputation. But if you were never in business before and you started a company after 40, I suppose it might be a little tougher. Either way, it's always possible to succeed, as long as you're not afraid of hard work."

Vernon K. Krieble (1885–1964)

LOCTITE CORPORATION

"Work is too much fun to give up."

It was Hartford's first real heat wave of the summer. The small group of alumni gathered at the Trinity College field house on that June day in 1955 were hoping that old Vernon Krieble would finally stop talking, so they could unwind in a cooler, more comfortable setting.

Ignoring the oppressive temperature, Krieble continued to extol the tremendous commercial potential of his new invention, an "anaerobic sealant," which, unlike any other adhesive then on the market, was capable of hardening in the absence of air. Having just retired from the school's chemistry department, the 70-year-old professor was starting a business to manufacture his invention.

"This is your chance to get in on the ground floor," he declared to the group. "I'm offering you shares in my new company."

Some of those present, former students of Krieble's, accepted his offer, but no one put much faith in his wildly optimistic claims. "All of us admire Vernon Krieble," recalled one alumnus. "Few of us believe that this man of 70 really has a money-making project. We all want to help him with what we think is just a retirement hobby; so we buy his convertible debentures, tuck them away, and forget about them. We have all done our good deed."[1]

28. Professor Vernon Krieble at work at his Trinity College Laboratory. The 68-year-old chemist started what is now Loctite Corp. in 1953 in anticipation of his retirement from the school's faculty.

For many, the "good deed" turned out to be the shrewdest investment of their lives. The old professor's retirement hobby would grow into the Loctite Corporation, a $240 million Big Board company that sells high-performance industrial adhesives to the manufacturers of automobiles, appliances, farm equipment, and hundreds of other products. An original investor's $1000 note, purchased in 1955, was worth 120 times that amount 15 years later.

Even Vern Krieble himself would have found it difficult to envision this kind of success on that long-ago June day. A short, pudgy man with a smooth, bespectacled face and almost no hair on his very round head, the pipe-smoking Krieble looked more like the retired college professor he was than a captain of industry. Indeed, it is doubtful he ever would have started a business were it not for Trinity's policy of mandatory retirement at age 70.

"I know that I would be the most disagreeable retired cuss you ever saw," he once told an interviewer. "And then, work is too much fun to give up, provided you work for something worthwhile, which it has always been my good fortune to do."

The son of a Pennsylvania farmer, Krieble began his career in 1907 when he joined the chemistry department at McGill University in Montreal. In 1920, the Brown-educated chemist became the chairman of the small (two instructors and fifty students) chemistry department at Trinity College. During his long tenure at the Connecticut school, Krieble developed one of the most respected small-college chemistry departments in the nation. The department was the first to require original research for its master's degree thesis, and among the first to have its curriculum certified by the American Chemical Society. For many years, it ranked second in the number of papers published by its faculty.

Nevertheless, when Vernon Krieble started his sealant company, his career had been limited to academia. This lack of business experience would have been a handicap even if the 70-year-old professor planned to start a small company dealing in a product or service that was already established. But Krieble wanted to do much more; his intent was not simply to start a new company, but to pioneer an entirely new manufacturing concept.

Ever since the beginning of the Machine Age, manufacturers relied on screws, bolts, and other "mechanical fasteners" to join metal parts to machinery. This method of attaching metal to metal had its problems—screws were always coming loose and falling off—but these were accepted as unavoidable consequences of engine vibrations. No one had ever given serious thought to developing a better way to join metal parts. Mechanical fasteners were as as much a part of modern industrial life as the assembly line.

Vernon Krieble planned to challenge the status quo with his new "chemical fastener." Krieble's bright red, resin-based sealant was ideally suited for use in the airless environment between machine parts because in addition to its anaerobic property of hardening in the absence of oxygen it formed an extremely strong bond on metal surfaces. Unlike mechanical fasteners, this bond could not be loosened by machine vibrations. It would not rust, leak, or need replacement, and because it was liquid, the sealant adapted itself perfectly to the contour of the metal parts it joined, resulting in a tighter fit and less intense vibrations. What's more, Krieble's invention eliminated the problem of loose screws falling into the machine engine, where they could cause serious damage.

Despite these advantages, the weight of tradition was solidly against Krieble's chemical fastener. Mechanical fasteners had been around for generations and had done at least an adequate job. The concept of a chemical sealant was alien to manufacturing engineers, almost all of whom doubted that any "glue" would be strong enough to withstand the stress of high-speed machines.

Selling Loctite to a skeptical industrial market would require much patient effort in order to educate manufacturers on the advantages of chemical fastening. As a former professor with almost a half century's experience explaining complex chemical reactions to undergraduates, Vernon Krieble was well equipped to meet this challenge. "Professor Krieble had a remarkable ability to take a difficult concept and make it understandable to anyone," said his son, early associate, and eventual successor, Dr. Robert Krieble. "This ability served him very well during Loctite's early years, when he had to explain a new and unknown technology to potential customers as well as to the salesmen we hired."

Ironically, Vernon Krieble did not become interested in the subject of chemical sealants until his career as a professor was almost over. His main area of academic interest had been the hydrolysis of sugars, organic nitriles, amides, and amygdalins. It was not until 1952, three years before his retirement, that he began to research anaerobic adhesives at the urging of his son Robert.

The technical director of General Electric's chemical materials laboratory in Pittsfield, Massachusetts, Dr. Krieble, a chemist like his father, was responsible for reviewing the sales potential of products developed by GE researchers. Among these products was an anaerobic permafil that hardened in the absence of air. Invented in 1945, the permafil was too unstable chemically to gain acceptance as a commercial product. Elaborate mixing and heating were required before it could be applied, and air had to be pumped constantly through the sealant during storage to keep it from turning rock hard for lack of oxygen. Seven years after its introduction, the permafil was being sold to only six regular customers. GE management had seen enough. The sealant was dropped from the company's line, over the objections of Robert Krieble, who still believed in its potential.

During a visit home in 1952, Robert Krieble discussed the

abandoned permafil with his father. Professor Krieble agreed that the sealant could be turned into a successful commercial product if it were made more stable chemically. With an eye toward his impending retirement, Vernon Krieble began to experiment with the unusual sealant, hoping to develop it into a product that could be used as the basis for his own business. He put in long hours at his Trinity College laboratory during the next year, looking for a way to stabalize the anaerobic permafil. He added different hydroperoxides to the original formula to find an effective thermal stabilizer, mixed in thickeners for viscosity, and introduced thixotropic agents for flow control. Later, he found that an oxygen-permeable polyethylene bottle could be used to keep the sealant from hardening during storage.

By 1953, Krieble had a stable, commercially practical, anaerobic sealant. Taking $800 in capital, he formed the American Sealants Company to test-market the product in the Hartford area under the name "Loctite." The response to the sealant from local manufacturers was encouraging, and by the time he retired in 1955, Krieble was ready to market Loctite on a larger scale. Doing this would require much more money than the professor, who had already spent $20,000 of his savings to develop the product, had at his disposal. To finance his expanded marketing effort, Krieble raised $115,000 from a group of ninety investors, many of them Trinity faculty, staff, and alumni.

With his product developed, capital raised, and a small, but solid, customer base established, Vernon Krieble was just about ready to shift his company into high gear. Before he did this, however, he needed an "inside man" who could handle the administrative and production end of the business while he put his experience to use where it would be most effective—educating potential customers.

The ideal candidate for the job was his son Bob.

Dr. Robert Krieble's initial reaction to his father's proposition was, "Holy smoke!" Although he too had been intrigued by the idea of a stable anaerobic sealant, the younger Krieble had never given much thought to his father's new business venture. "I was making $35,000 a year at GE, which was a considerable sum back then. It certainly wasn't the kind of money that one just walked away from, least of all when one had two children about to start boarding school."

Still, Bob Krieble wanted to get out from under the weight of a big corporation. "The idea of being in business with my father appealed to me. I was impressed that he was getting repeat business, because this showed the product was working in commercial applications. He had also raised a great deal of money, and his enthusiasm was contagious. I brought the matter up with my wife [Nancy], and she said, "Go ahead. You're 39, and if you don't do it now, you never will. Then you might regret it.'"

On June 15, 1956, Bob Krieble was named vice-president of American Sealants Company. (The corporate name was changed to Loctite seven years later). His annual salary was $12,000.

Blending their divergent talents into a harmonious partnership, father and son built a successful business. In fiscal 1958, the company showed its first profit, $27,311, on sales of $174,233. By fiscal 1961, Robert Krieble's fifth anniversary with the firm, profits climbed to $153,000. One year later, the company paid its first cash dividend.

The Kriebles were able to realize an excellent profit on the sale of their sealant, because they set prices high in relation to production costs. "The customer was able to save a great deal of money by using our product, and we charged him according to

29. A memorial window in the Trinity College chemistry building honors Vernon Krieble's invention of a stable one-part anaerobic sealant.

205

this usage rather than our costs," explained Robert Krieble. "There was one prospective customer, the owner of an outboard motor company, who didn't want to buy from us because he said our price was too high. Professor Krieble said to him, 'I'll tell you what, I'll give you the sealant for free if you agree to pay us 10 percent of whatever it saves you in production costs.' The man ended up buying Loctite at our price.

As his business prospered, Professor Krieble (who remained president of Loctite until his death in 1964) remembered Trinity College with generous donations. In 1959, he made his first contribution to the school on behalf of the company. In a note to Trinity president Albert C. Jacobs, he thanked the school for allowing him to start his business in the chemistry building, describing the experience as a "great boon to one who has refused to accept that at the age of 70 one's mind shrivels and dies."[2]

George W. Plumly (1909–)

PLUMLY INDUSTRIES

*"People will always say it can't be done,
until someone comes along and does it."*

"In almost every fight I ever won, I had to come back after being knocked down."

The speaker is George Plumly, a successful manufacturer of aviation and industrial lighting systems. A tough 77-year-old Texan, Plumly is not speaking metaphorically. In the late 1920s, he made his living as a professional welterweight boxer.

"I was pretty good," said Plumly, who fought under the name "Young Webb." "For a time I was ranked in the top ten in my division. I fought Barney Ross twice and lost both times, but I did beat some of the top contenders of my day."

Plumly's last fight against Ross, in the autumn of 1929, earned him a $3000 paycheck. Taking $1100 of his winnings, he treated himself to "an early Christmas present," enrolling in a Cincinnati flying school.

"My first flight was on Christmas Day, 1929, and from that point on I have been hooked on flying," he recalled in an old country-preacher voice.

More than three decades later, Plumly turned his love for aviation into an immensely profitable business, when, at 53, he started Plumly Industries in the garage of his Fort Worth home. The bald, muscular entrepreneur pioneered an impressive series of aircraft lighting innovations at Plumly Industries between 1962 and 1987; among them were a glare-free chart holder that illuminates navigational charts without upsetting the pilot's night vision, and the first Federal Aviation Administration (FAA)-approved floor-proximity emergency lighting system designed to help passengers find their way out of a smoke-filled cabin.

Royalties from these and over a hundred other inventions net George Plumly a personal income reputed to be in the neighborhood of $1 million a year. He and his wife of 43 years, Mildred, live in a modern lakeside mansion outside Fort Worth that is equipped with a complete gym, where Plumly works out daily. He also owns a Cessna 401 that he still pilots himself.

The life of a Sunbelt millionaire is a far cry from George Plumly's rugged beginnings in the Midwest. Born in Chillicothe, Ohio, in 1909, Plumly was forced to leave home by his father, a railroad worker, when he was only 14.

"I don't know how to put this ... but my father hated children," he said. "Psychologists probably have a word for this sort of behavior today, but back then we just accepted it. My father was a pretty vengeful man, and believe me, he wasn't shy about expressing his vengeance. When I was 14, my mother suggested it might be a good idea if I left home; a few years later the same thing happened to my younger sister."

Plumly did not see his father again until 1945, at his mother's funeral. "I saw him one time after that, and then he passed away and I went to his funeral. Looking back, I feel kind of sorry for him. He was raised in a family where the grandmother was the dominant member, and he was the only boy, with five sisters. When he was 18, he went to work for the railroad and stayed there until he was 65, working 10 hours a day, six days a week."

Out on his own, Plumly survived by peddling Dover irons and other appliances to the residents of small Ohio communities during the early days of rural electrification. He obtained appliances from the Dayton Power and Light Company and sold them to residents along the newly laid power lines.

Along the way, Plumly managed to complete high school. He also learned how to box, and in 1928 his skill in the sport earned him a partial scholarship to the University of Cincinnati. "I always wanted to get an education, because I believed this was the way to better myself," he later recalled. "My first goal was to become a surgeon, but since I didn't think I'd ever have the money for medical school, I settled on becoming an engineer."

The scholarship did not come close to covering all of Plumly's expenses, and to make ends meet he fought professionally under the Young Webb alias. This, of course, was in direct violation of the amateur rules of college sports, and when the university learned of its star boxer's extracurricular activities, he was dismissed from the team.

With his scholarship cut off, Plumly turned to the professional ring full time. He quit boxing about two years later, because "it hurt too much," but nevertheless he credits the sport with teaching him a valuable lesson that he later used to succeed in business.

"In boxing, you learn how to lose as well as how to win. This is sure something that you better know if you want to be an entrepreneur, because things are never going to go your way all the time. I'm lucky if one out of ten of the projects I work on ever makes it to the marketplace. I've seen a lot of people start a business with big ideas, but the minute things get tough they run; they obviously weren't cut out to be entrepreneurs."

Plumly had plenty of experience dealing with adversity after he left boxing in the early 1930s. Living in Cincinnati, he struggled at a variety of menial jobs, spending most of his money on engineering courses and his ever-increasing interest in aviation. For a time, he lived in a Cincinnati airport hangar to save on rent.

His first real break came in 1933, when he became an appliance buyer for L. S. Ayres department store in Indianapolis. Plumly's career advanced steadily over the remainder of the decade; he became head appliance buyer for J. L. Hudson in Detroit in 1936 and three years later was named sales manager of Hoosier Kitchen Furniture, a New Castle, Indiana, manufacturer of tables and cabinets.

At Hoosier Kitchen, Plumly exhibited his first talent as an inventor. Looking for a novelty item that he could give to architects and builders, who were his main customers, he created a pencil with a thin, straight edge that could be used for precision drafting. After World War II, this invention became known throughout the world as the mechanical pencil.

Despite the success of the pencil, it netted Plumly only $300 in royalties. Looking back almost 50 years later, the millionaire inventor recalled his pencil contract blunder and the lesson it taught him. "I patented the pencil in 1940, and for a brief time had it made for me by a jeweler in Muncie. Then the jeweler sold his store, and so I signed a contract with the Dixon Write Right Company of Chicago, which entitled me to receive a half-cent royalty on every twelfth pencil the company sold for a period of five years.

"Then right after we made the deal, Pearl Harbor happened and Dixon stopped making pencils. By the time the war ended, the five-year contract was just about up and the rights to the pencil belonged to Dixon. They licensed Parker and other companies around the world to manufacture the pencil after the war, and everybody got rich but me."

The pencil experience didn't bring Plumly wealth, but it did teach him a valuable lesson. "Ever since that time, I've never signed anything without legal advice, and I've never gotten involved in a project unless I am sure that it is, one, patentable, and, two, it has at least some chance, however small, of making money. We are not cloud nine people around here."

According to Plumly, an invention has to meet at least one of two criteria to have a chance at commercial success: it must save people money or do a job better than anything currently on the market. "Success is never guaranteed," he cautioned, "but if you can help people stretch their dollars or make their lives easier, you'll increase the odds in your favor."

George Plumly created new products that did both of these things when he worked for the Frigidaire division of General Motors in the years following the war. Among his more notable inventions at Frigidaire were the quick-release ice cube tray ("the metal ones with the lever"), sliding and revolving refrigerator shelves, and the integrated faucet, which allowed hot and cold water to flow out of the same tap.

"Before this, you had separate taps for hot and cold water," said Plumly. "When I proposed to design one tap for hot and cold water, everyone on the engineering staff told me it couldn't be done, so I had to take the project home and begin working on it in my own workshop. But that's how it goes; people will always say something can't be done, until someone comes along and does it."

During his three years with GM, Plumly became acquainted with Charles "Boss" Kettering, inventor of the self-starting engine and founder of GM's Delco division, which, like Frigidaire, was headquartered in Dayton. Kettering gave his younger GM colleague some advice that struck a responsive chord in Plumly.

"Boss Kettering was one of the greatest inventors of this century, so when he talked you listened. One thing that he would tell other inventors was, 'Get off and travel on the side road, because if you stay on the main road, you're only going to see things that have been done before.'"

In 1952, Plumly, then 43, left GM to follow his own side road as a manufacturer's representative of aircraft parts. This led to a very well paying job as sales manager of Wyman-Gordon, the Worcester, Massachusetts, manufacturer of heavy industrial equipment.

"The Wyman-Gordon offer was too good for me to turn down," said Plumly. "After a few years, though, I decided that I had to go back on my own. I knew that I was never going to want to retire, and I didn't ever want to be in the position of being told that I had to step down at 65 because of some company policy.

"My family discouraged me from quitting my job. Everybody wants security rather than opportunity, and they were no different."

Plumly left Wyman-Gordon in 1962 and, at 53, started Plumly Industries. His first product was a hand-held "logarithmic calculator" for pilots; he followed this with a nylon flight bag, before scoring his first major success with the illuminated chart holder in 1963.

Like many of Plumly's inventions, the chart holder came about as a result of his personal experience. "Once I was flying into LaGuardia at night during a pretty bad storm, and every time I put the flashlight on my navigational charts, the glare would blind me for a few seconds. I vowed that if I ever got back on the ground alive, I'd find a better way to illuminate charts."

Plumly's chart holder, which utilizes a series of conical lights arranged to reflect inward, succeeded in illuminating charts without casting a distracting glare in the flight cabin. The chart holder has become standard in military and general aviation. It is used on all planes assigned to the White House, all FAA-owned and -operated aircraft, over 10,000 military planes, and many Fortune 500 corporate jets.

Getting the chart holder accepted by the military initially, however, proved to be a near-impossible task, requiring a most unusual demonstration of the product to General Curtis LeMay. After being frustrated by the Pentagon bureaucracy for months, Plumly began to pester LeMay's secretary, until he finally was given an appointment to show his invention to the general. When he arrived at LeMay's office, he was dismayed by what he saw: three of the walls were covered with unshaded windows, and the room was bathed in Washington sunlight. It was hardly the best spot to demonstrate a new lighting device!

Confronted with this situation, Plumly came up with his unusual demonstration. "I asked, 'General, are you overly proud?' He said, 'No.' 'Then, let's you and me crawl under your desk where it's dark, so I can show you this lighted chart holder.' We got under the desk, and he said, 'Jesus Christ'—those were his very words—'this is a good deal. I want one for my plane right away.' I said to him, 'General, I didn't come up here to sell you one light. How the hell do I sell your air force?'"

Plumly followed the chart holder with a series of nonaviation inventions, including an improved, low-wattage version of the traditional "exit sign" for commercial buildings, and the Disto-Map, a device that allows motorists to determine the driving distances between cities by turning a disc.

After being successfully developed and marketed for a time, both of these inventions were sold to larger companies: the exit sign to Cooper Industries and the Disto-Map to Rand McNally. This is typical of the way Plumly Industries operated under George Plumly. It created new, patentable products, proved their marketability, and then sold the rights to them to a larger manufacturer.

"As a small, entrepreneurial company, we're better able to develop a new product," Plumly said. "The bigger companies, on the other hand, are often better at manufacturing and distributing it. We incur a lot of costs in developing the product, and we like to recover this investment in up-front money when we sell the rights to it. Then we'll make our profits on royalties."

Plumly's most recent invention is the Plumly Advanced Incandescent Emergency Egress Lighting System for commercial aircraft. The system was introduced in response to an FAA ruling requiring that all commercial aircraft with seats for fifteen passengers or more be equipped with emergency exit lighting positioned no higher than four feet off the floor (smoke rises). The FAA ruling, which went into effect on November 26, 1986, was issued in the aftermath of a tragedy that occurred three-and-a-half years earlier, when twenty-three people died in a fire in an Air Canada DC-9 that had just landed at the Cincinnati airport, because dense smoke prevented them from locating the exits.

The Plumly lighting system, the first of its kind approved by the FAA, lights up the floor of an airplane cabin like a runway, outlining the aisle with white lights and marking the exits with red lights. Unlike the ambient lights traditionally used in aircraft, which are incapable of penetrating dense smoke, Plumly's floor-mounted incandescent filaments are visible for up to 100 feet in an environment of 90 percent smoke density.

But the demand for Plumly's emergency egress lighting failed

30. George Plumly, inventor, entrepreneur, and former professional boxer, was still piloting his own corporate jet in 1986, as he approached his seventy-eighth birthday. (*Photo by David Lindsey*)

to meet his expectations, a development he attributes to a "vendetta" on the part of major airlines. "The airlines were against the FAA requirement because of its cost, but we agitated for it, so now they're punishing us." In May 1987, while his wife was recovering from a serious operation, Plumly sold some of his lighting patents and "suspended" operations at Plumly Industries, forming in its place G. P. Lighting Corp., a small research firm. Nevertheless, he remains as intrepid as ever. He has initiated patent infringement suits against competing manufacturers of emergency lighting and talks confidently of reviving Plumly Industries. The thought of retirement seems far away. "Why should I retire? Business is a game to me; I do it because it's fun. The money is very secondary."

Carl G. Sontheimer (1914–   )

CUISINART, INC.

"If you aren't passionate . . . don't even bother."

When Carl Sontheimer retired in 1969 he was "overjoyed" by the prospect of never having to work again. An MIT-trained research physicist, the 55-year-old Greenwich, Connecticut, man had netted a handsome profit on the sale of his engineering firm, and he looked forward to spending the rest of his life in idle comfort.

But Sontheimer soon grew restless with the uneventful routine of retired life. In 1970, the bored former executive began casting about for a new business opportunity.

He first considered starting a firm to sell home security systems. This would have been a sound business decision; the spiraling crime rate had scared many homeowners into seeking out new ways of protecting their property. But Sontheimer was interested in more than the bottom line. Already well-off financially, he wanted a business that could deliver emotional, as well as monetary, rewards.

"I was quite certain that my idea for a home security business would work, but in actuality I wasn't terribly excited by it, so I dropped the whole thing," he recalled. "As an engineer, I learned a long time ago that if you aren't passionate about a project, then you shouldn't even bother starting it; because at some point you will run up against a major obstacle, and without passion you will not have the tenacity to overcome that obstacle."

One thing that Sontheimer was passionate about was cooking, particularly French cooking. This interest dated back to a childhood spent in Paris, after his father was transferred to France to become the export sales manager of an American paint company. As a young man just out of college, he became a serious student of the culinary arts, building up an impressive collection of cookbooks and corresponding with famous chefs like Julia Child.

Sontheimer decided to convert his avocation into a retirement business by becoming a cooking teacher; but this venture came to an abrupt end when he discovered that he was "all thumbs" in front of a class. ("I simply could not talk and demonstrate to students at the same time without making a royal mess.")

The former physicist then tried food journalism. "I wrote articles for a nationally *unknown* publication, *The Westport* [Connecticut] *Free Press*. This was great fun, but it really wasn't enough to keep me occupied, so I convinced my wife, Shirley, to go with me to a trade show in France, where I hoped to find a line of French cookware to import to this country."

In 1971, the Sontheimers went to the French show, where Carl indeed signed a contract to become the exclusive U.S. importer for a cookware firm. Before leaving the show, Sontheimer chanced upon another product—one that he would ultimately make famous as the Cuisinart food processor.

"At one of the exhibits we visited, we saw a most unique machine called the Robot Coupe food processor," he recounted. "It had been developed only a few years earlier by a gentleman named Pierre Verdum; and, in essence, it was the first true food processor in the world."

Verdum was interested in marketing his invention only to the restaurant trade, but Sontheimer recognized its potential as a household kitchen appliance. The two men talked, and "within minutes" they agreed to a deal: Verdum would build a modified version of the machine, making it smaller and safe for domestic use, and Sontheimer would sell it in this country as its sole U.S. importer. They further agreed that the food processor would be marketed in America under the label "Cuisinart," a name coined by Sontheimer.

Getting the Cuisinart food processor established in America proved to be far more difficult than Sontheimer had imagined. The modifications that Verdum had made in his restaurant machine were not extensive enough to meet the safety standards of United Laboratories, which refused to grant "UL approval" to the home food processor.

Here was a major obstacle, the kind that Carl Sontheimer had known would inevitably confront any new venture. Had this been a home security business, he might have accepted his losses and gone on to something new. But as an amateur chef, Sontheimer was too enthusiastic about the idea of a home food processor to be deterred by the UL rejection. Having worked on the development of many scientific instruments during his engineering career, he was able to add the necessary safety features to the Cuisinart's design. (He would eventually patent a dozen improvements in the food processor.)

In 1973, a UL-approved Cuisinart was finally ready for the American market. Sontheimer introduced the food processor at the January housewares show in Chicago. No sooner had the machine been unveiled, however, than he encountered another major obstacle.

"When I introduced the food processor in Chicago, three of the reps who were selling our French cookware line quit on the spot. They said that I was absolutely crazy to think that I could sell this funny-looking small appliance for over a hundred dollars." (In the late sixties and early seventies, small appliances like toasters and blenders rarely fetched more than forty or fifty dollars.)

It seemed for a time as if Sontheimer's ex-sales reps were right. Although department store buyers were favorably impressed by the Cuisinart, no one wanted to be the first to gamble on the unusual kitchen appliance with the unusually high price tag. "That's a great machine, but come back when you have some solid sales figures to show us," was the response that invariably followed Sontheimer's demonstrations of the food processor.

Unable to penetrate the department store market, Sontheimer concentrated on selling his product to independent gourmet shops. He garnered valuable publicity for the food processor by demonstrating it to the editors of *Gourmet,* who ran a favorable feature on the machine, complete with a full-color photograph. A short time later, Craig Claiborne wrote an article on the Cuisinart, hailing it as a "miracle machine."

More valuable to Cuisinart than this publicity was the dramatic rise in the popularity of gourmet cooking in the mid-1970s. Almost every major newspaper of the time expanded its food section; cookbook and gourmet magazine sales reached unprecedented heights; and countless home cooks, who had previously limited their efforts to standard American dishes, suddenly began experimenting with continental specialities like quiche and fondue.

Against this backdrop, the Cuisinart food processor emerged as one of the retail stars of the decade. Department stores that earlier had refused even to carry the machine began to feature it in heavily advertised sales, knowing that its notoriety would attract large crowds of housewares shoppers. (Ironically, the Cuisinart's popularity as a "department store special" made it virtually impossible for the independent gourmet shops, who had pioneered the product, to continue carrying it, since they could not compete with the low sale prices charged by their big competitors.)

Sontheimer's success led established appliance makers like General Electric, Sunbeam, and Waring to come out with their own food processors. These competitors kept their prices as much as 75 percent below Cuisinart's, but such was the reputation of Sontheimer's machine that it continued to capture a 60 percent share of the market.

The power of the Cuisinart mystique was vividly demonstrated during the 1977 Christmas season, when Sontheimer, his supply of product temporarily cut off by a dock strike, marketed a gift box containing a food processor blade and a certificate guaranteeing delivery of a complete machine at a later date for $225. Despite the grumblings of some department stores, who objected to selling a "promise and an empty carton," consumers purchased over 60,000 of the gift boxes.

Sontheimer capitalized on the ever-increasing popularity of his food processor by putting the Cuisinart label on other products, such as meat thermometers, metric beam scales, glass-domed convection ovens, and croissant cutters. He also began publication of his own monthly magazine, *Cooking*, in February 1978, fea-

turing stories by some of the world's foremost chefs and gour-
mets.

Building a "postretirement business" on a French product
represented a homecoming of sorts for Carl Sontheimer, some
of whose happiest memories are of the seven childhood years he
spent in Paris.

"I was 11 when my family moved from New York to France,
and I became assimilated very quickly. The French people accepted me right away—there was absolutely no resentment over
my being American. I remember waking up one day and discovering that I had suddenly become quite fluent in French; so
fluent, in fact, that I subsequently won several prizes in French
composition. Even today, I doubt that any Frenchman who had
met me only through an exchange of letters would suspect that
I am not French. Of course, I do speak the language with an
accent, though no one can place it as American."

In 1932 Sontheimer left France and returned to the United
States and MIT to earn his degree in physics. After graduation,
he became a research engineer for several companies, including
RCA, and patented over twenty inventions in the field of electronics.

Sontheimer earned a comfortable income as a corporate sci-
entist, but the desire for greater creative freedom eventually led
him to choose a more entrepreneurial career. "By 1946 I noticed
that a distinct pattern had emerged in my professional life; I got
along famously with the people who reported to me, but I had
all kinds of trouble with management. The only solution to this
problem was for me to be my own boss, so I became an independent consultant engineer.

"I had $2500 in the bank, a wife and three children to sup-
port," continued Sontheimer. "My plan was to go with my own
consulting business until my savings ran out. I was confident that
I could quickly obtain another good job should that happen, since
I was fairly well known in engineering circles and, in fact, was
always getting attractive job offers."

Sontheimer's savings account never ran dry. His consulting
business prospered, and within a year he expanded it into CGS
Laboratories, an engineering firm specializing in electronic mea-
suring and radio receiving instruments. At CGS, he developed a
communications device for the military that would later find a

new application in the civilian market as the automatic station scanner on car radios.

But even in his own company, Sontheimer had trouble getting along with "management." He left CGS in 1960, following a dispute with his investors, and founded ANZAC, a firm that made lightweight, high-frequency microwave components. Sontheimer sold ANZAC to Adams-Russell, Inc., of Waltham, Massachusetts, in 1967 and remained with the company as a group vice-president for two more years before beginning his short-lived retirement.

Looking back on his career in his seventy-second year, the hulking, rumpled Sontheimer dismissed any notion of retiring for a second time. "I doubt that I will ever retire. My wife and I keep very busy running Cuisinart, and we enjoy it."

Indeed, the Sontheimers have taken on even more responsibilities with the passage of time. Since 1980, they have overseen the design and production of all food processors bearing the Cuisinart label. This followed a lengthy and often bitter dispute with Robot Coupe, which began when Pierre Verdum sold the French firm in 1976.

"We had an excellent relationship with Pierre Verdum, but when he sold Robot Coupe to a very large French company, the quality of the machines began to drop perceptibly," said Sontheimer. "What's more, the company refused to make any improvements in the machine's design, putting us in danger of falling behind some of our new competitors.

"This was something we simply couldn't tolerate, so in 1978 we started designing and building some of the models in the Cuisinart line ourselves. Two years later we reached an agreement with Robot Coupe that gave us all rights to the Cuisinart name; since then every Cuisinart food processor made has been engineered by our company."

How would Sontheimer describe the food processor's role in the modern kitchen? "It is the single most important appliance I have ever seen," he snapped. Fifteen years after discovering the machine at a French trade show, he was still passionate.

Advice

In every interview we conducted for this book, we asked our subject two questions:

- What advice would you give to other post-40 entrepreneurs who are starting their own businesses?
- Do you feel that being over 40 has any effect—good or bad—on an entrepreneur's chances of achieving success?

The following is a sampling of the answers we received:

Willis K. Drake—Data Card Corporation

My advice to an entrepreneur of any age is to get an outside, objective view of his idea's market potential. It's not enough simply to have a good idea; it has to fit into the marketplace. The entrepreneur is often too close to his planned business to evaluate it objectively, so he should seek advice from someone whose judgment he respects. The older entrepreneur has an advantage here, because he has more of an overview and is more likely to seek outside counsel than the younger entrepreneur, who often just wants to plow ahead.

Tom Duck—Ugly Duckling Rent-A-Car System, Inc.

Don't be embarrassed about starting any business at any age; you're never too old to do it.

Wilbert L. Gore—W. L. Gore & Associates

Be lucky. . . . Have adequate capital. . . . Find a niche where there's a need not being filled. . . . Avoid highly competitive markets. . . . And be willing to put in *lots* of hours.

John K. Hanson—Winnebago Industries, Inc.

Use your past experience and education to find an opportunity. The opportunities are always there, often right under your own nose. A lot of people get too caught up in looking at the national scene, and they miss the chance to start a good local or regional business. When you do start a business, be sure to keep a foot in the back door. Never risk it all; always leave yourself a way out.

Murray J. Harpole—Pentair, Inc.

There are some benefits that result from one's maturity, but age is not a really important factor in entrepreneurship. My advice to all entrepreneurs is: be sure that you are prepared to make a commitment of some significant duration during which you will expend all of your time and energy to make the business succeed. You have to expect that the first three years are going to be very shaky and very difficult. You should be sure that you have the support of your family, or be prepared to lose your family, because a business start-up will put a strain on all of you. My other piece of advice is to be flexible enough to adapt your plans to a changing reality. There are so many things outside of your control, you are going to have to modify your plans as you proceed.

Frank D. Hickingbotham—TCBY Enterprises, Inc.

Age is an attitude. The point in life that you begin a venture is inconsequential; it's the confidence in your ability and the timeliness of your idea. You also need to be committed to the success of your associates if you want your business to grow.

Bill LeVine—Postal Instant Press

You have to make a lot of personal sacrifices when you start a business, regardless of your age. When you work for someone else, your family comes first, but when you start a business, your business comes first. It's building the future for your family.

Perry Mendel—Kinder-Care Learning Centers, Inc.

You can't get big if you try to handle every little detail yourself. You have to find good people and delegate. Of course, you have to be prepared to work long and hard, too, so you'd better love your work. Age is no factor in determining how much an entre-preneur can do as long as he's motivated. I feel better today than I did at 46, when I started Kinder-Care.

David A. Norman—Businessland, Inc.

I don't know that age makes any difference in business. Success is a matter of mental attitude. You have to be persistent, you have to focus in on your goals, and you have to be flexible enough to change as your situation changes. It's also critical to surround yourself with good people, both in your work environment and on the board level.

George W. Plumly—Plumly Industries

Don't go into anything that isn't compatible with your previous work experience; there will be too many surprises. Don't burn any bridges that you don't have to, even if it means keeping your old job as you start your business. Make sure you have enough money to carry you through for at least one year, because every-thing will take longer to accomplish than you anticipated.

John Psarouthakis—J. P. Industries, Inc.

First, you have to be sure that you are truly prepared to take the risk of going out on your own. There are many men and women in the upper levels of corporations today who are capable of doing what I have done, but they cannot pull themselves away from the apparent security of a big corporation. Success is avail-able if you are willing to take it.

Alfred J. Roach—TII Industries, Inc.

Have a realistic time limit. If your idea doesn't work, get the hell out and try something else. Don't worry about failing. As far as age goes, it's absolutely easier to start a successful business when you're over 40, because you have the experience.

Carl G. Sontheimer—Cuisinart, Inc.

Before you start a company, define in one sentence what you want your customers to think of you. When I started Cuisinart, I wrote, "When a home cooking enthusiast wants a new piece of equipment, I want the first thought that comes to her mind to be 'Does Cuisinart make it?' "

Notes

Preface (pp. vii–xi)

1. U.S. Bureau of the Census, *Current Population Reports,* Series P-25, No. 937.

Introduction: Age Assets (pp. 1–5)

1. Business Economics Division, Dun & Bradstreet, Inc., *The Business Failure Report* (1984 final, 1985 preliminary), (New York: Dun & Bradstreet, Inc., 1985).

Frank D. Hickingbotham (pp. 9–15)

1. Carol E. Curtis, "All Pleasure, No Guilt," *Forbes,* 25 March 1985, p. 198.
2. Ibid.

Bill LeVine (pp. 16–22)

1. "Secrets of Winners: Postal Instant Press," *The Franchise Advisor,* July 1986, p. 51.

David Mullany (pp. 23–29)

1. Steven Levy, "The Wiffle Ball," *Esquire,* August 1983, p. 83.

Jacob L. Barowsky (pp. 47–52)

1. Hal Meden, "Lestoil's Four Fabulous TV Years," *Sponsor,* 15 February 1958.
2. Jacob Barowsky, "The Story of Lestoil," Address to the Advertising & Sales Club of Toronto, 10 November 1959.

3. "Can Lestoil Repel Muscular Ad Threats by Big Three's All-Purpose Detergents?" *Printers' Ink,* 24 July 1959, p. 12.

Roy J. Carver (pp. 53–58)

1. "Sedco Case Plaintiff Seeks $17 Million," *New York Times,* 23 September 1980, sec. IV.
2. Ibid.

John K. Hanson (pp. 59–65)

1. "The Forbes Four Hundred," *Forbes,* Fall 1983, p. 112.

Perry Mendel (pp. 75–81)

1. Geoffrey Smith, "Perry Mendel's Golden Diapers," *Forbes,* 25 June 1979, p. 68.
2. Joseph Lelyveld, "Drive-In Day Care," *New York Times* Sunday Magazine, 5 June 1977, p. 110.

William H. Millard (pp. 82–88)

1. "The Forbes Four Hundred," *Forbes,* 1 October 1984, p. 86.
2. Ibid.
3. Deborah C. Wise, "How To Sell Computers Today and How Not To," *Business Week,* 2 September 1985, p. 72.
4. Pauline Yoshihashi, "A Daughter's Quick Rise to the Top," *New York Times,* 16 December 1984, sec. III.

Lowell W. Paxson and Roy M. Speer (pp. 89–95)

1. Michael Winerip, "TV Shopping Brings the Mall to the Home," *New York Times,* 27 April 1986, sec. I.
2. James Cox, "Airing Deals for Armchair Shoppers," *USA Today,* 7 August 1986, sec. B.
3. Peter J. Boyer, "Going to the Mall on Cable TV," *New York Times,* 13 June 1986, sec. D.
4. Ibid.
5. "The Four Hundred Richest People in America," *Forbes,* 27 October 1986, p. 168.
6. Dale Kasler, "Merchandise Is the Message," *Tampa Tribune,* 8 June 1986, sec. E.
7. James Cox, "TV's Discount Hawkers Losing Millions," *USA Today,* 19 February 1987, sec. A.

Ralph E. Schneider (pp. 96–101)

1. The Editors of the *Wall Street Journal, The New Millionaires and How They Made It* (New York: Bernard Geis Associates, 1960), p. 94.
2. Ibid., p. 95.

David A. Norman (pp. 105–111)

1. Tom Quinlan, "1985 Is a Year of Vindication for Businessland's David Norman," *Computer Retail News,* 18 November 1985, p. 149.
2. Deborah C. Wise, "How To Sell Computers Today and How Not To," *Business Week,* 2 September 1985, pp. 70 and 72.

William C. Norris (pp. 112–118)

1. Gregory H. Wierzynski, "Control Data's Newest Cliffhanger," *Fortune,* February 1968, p. 127.
2. "Control Data: Is There Room for Change After Bill Norris?" *Business Week,* 17 October 1983, p. 121.
3. Patrick Houston, "Control Data's Struggle to Come Back From the Brink," ibid., 14 October 1985, p. 63.

Sam A. Sarno (pp. 119–125)

1. Mary Ann Linsen, "High-Flying Coupons Soar to the Skies," *Progressive Grocer,* February 1981, p. 65.
2. Robert H. Bork, "Getting Rich on Cents-Off Coupons," *Forbes* 16 January 1984, p. 62.

Robert F. de Graff (pp. 129–135)

1. John Tebbel, *A History of Book Publishing in the United States* (New York: R. R. Bowker, 1972), vol. III, p. 509.

Merle N. Norman (pp. 160–166)

1. Connie O'Kelley, *Merle Nethercutt Norman: An American Success Story* (Los Angeles: privately published, 1976), pp. 77 and 78.

Anthony T. Rossi (pp. 173–180)

1. Wayne King, "A Taste for Profits," *New York Times,* 16 June 1974, sec. III.

2. "The Would-Be Explorer Who Started Tropicana," *New York Times,* 16 January 1979, sec. IV.

3. Authors' interview with Anthony Rossi, Spring 1986.

Vernon K. Krieble (pp. 200–206)

1. Ellsworth S. Grant, *Drop by Drop* (Newington, CT: privately published, 1983), p. 22.

2. Ibid., p. 35.

Bibliography

Note: In researching virtually every biography, the authors relied primarily on interviews conducted with the subject and his or her associates and descendents. Secondary sources (books and articles) are listed in this bibliography according to their importance to the authors' research.

Barowsky, Jacob L.

Hal Meden, "Lestoil's Four Fabulous TV Years," *Sponsor,* 15 February 1958; Lawrence M. Hughes, "Spot TV in Four Years Sends Lestoil Soaring 56,000%," *Sales Management,* 21 February 1958, pp. 48–52; "Can Lestoil Repel Muscular Ad Threats by Big Three's All-Purpose Detergents?" *Printers' Ink,* 24 July 1959, pp. 11 and 12; Adeline Seamon Barowsky, *The Two of Us* (Holyoke, MA: privately published, 1985); Jacob Barowsky obituary, *New York Times,* 28 October 1977, sec. II; Jacob Barowsky, "The Story of Lestoil" (Address to the Advertising and Sales Club of Toronto, Toronto, Canada, 10 November 1959). The authors also obtained information used in this biography from a telephone interview conducted with Mr. Barowsky's son-in-law, Isaac Eskenasy, on 18 March 1986.

Carver, Roy J.

Arthur M. Louis, "New Rich of the Seventies," *Fortune,* September 1973, p. 170; Ruth Simon, "Minding the Store," *Forbes,* 4 November 1985, pp. 208–9; "Sedco Case Plaintiff Seeks $17 Million," *New York Times,* 23 September 1980, sec. IV; "Roy J. Carver Induction Into the Tire Industry Hall of Fame" (Pamphlet, National Tire Dealers and Retreaders Association Annual Convention, Atlanta, 21 September 1985). Most of the material used in the preparation of this biography was obtained from an interview with Mr. Carver's son, Martin Carver, on 17 April 1986.

de Graff, Robert F.

John Tebbel, *A History of Book Publishing in the United States* (New York: R. R. Bowker, 1972), vols. III and IV, s.v. "Pocket Books"; *Current Biography* (New York: H. W. Wilson & Co., 1943), s.v. "Robert de Graff"; "New 25¢ Books Offered," *New York Times,* 16 June 1939; "Little Book Battle," *Business Week,* 10 January 1942, p. 28; Freeman Lewis, "A Brief History of Pocket Books" (New York: privately published, 1967); Robert de Graff obituary, *New York Times,* 3 November 1981, sec. B. The authors conducted telephone interviews with Mr. de Graff's widow, Dorcas de Graff, and his former associate, Leon Shimkin, on 28 April 1986 and 20 October 1986, respectively.

Drake, Willis K.

"Data Card Corp: Profits From Plastic Cards," *Dunn's Review,* September 1978, pp. 22–23; James Cook, "A Neat Business," *Forbes,* 2 December 1985, p. 99; "It's All in the Cards," *Financial World,* 3–16 April 1985, p. 128. Most of the material used in the preparation of this biography was obtained during a personal interview the authors conducted with Mr. Drake on 27 March 1986.

Duck, Tom

John A. Byrne, "Keeping Out of Mischief Now," *Forbes,* 8 October 1984, pp. 238–39; "How to Ride a Recession," *New York Times,* 18 May 1980, sec. III; John A. Byrne, "It Ain't Over Until It's Over," *Forbes,* 15 July 1985, p. 104. Most of the material used in the preparation of this biography was obtained during a telephone interview the authors conducted with Mr. Duck on 17 April 1986.

Gore, Wilbert L.

Alex Ward, "An All-Weather Idea," *New York Times* Sunday magazine, 10 November 1985, pp. 68 and 86–87ff; Lucien Rhodes, "The Un-Manager," *Inc.,* August 1982, p. 34ff; Stanley W. Angrist, "Classless Capitalist," *Forbes,* 9 May 1983, pp. 122 and 124; Michael J. White, "The Gorey Details," *Management Review,* March 1985, pp. 16–17; "Excellence in Management Awards: Wilbert L. Gore," *Industry Week,* 17 October 1983, pp. 48–49; "Fabric Laminate Rides Fashion Wave," *New York Times,* 14 May 1984, sec. IV. The authors conducted a telephone interview with Wilbert and Vieve Gore on 4 April 1986.

Hanson, John K.

"Striking It Rich in Forest City," *Forbes*, 1 June 1972, pp. 37–39; "Winnebago Turns to Other Products," *New York Times*, 30 September 1980, sec. IV; Jay Gissen, "Good Times in Forest City," *Forbes*, 13 February 1984, p. 66; "The Winnebago Story" (Forest City, Iowa: privately published, 1983). "The Forbes Four Hundred," *Forbes*, Fall 1983, p. 112. Information used in the preparation of this biography was also obtained from a telephone interview the authors conducted with Mr. Hanson on 31 January 1986.

Harpole, Murray J.

Del Marth, "Friendly Takeovers," *Nation's Business*, May 1986, pp. 93–94; and Lynda McDonnell, "Minnesota Power, Pentair Partnership Makes It Come True," *St. Paul Pioneer Press Dispatch*, 9 March 1986. The authors obtained most of the material used in this biography from a telephone interview with Mr. Harpole on 16 July 1986.

Hickingbotham, Frank D.

Carol E. Curtis, "All Pleasure, No Guilt," *Forbes*, 25 March 1985, pp. 194 and 198; Bob Sharpe, "3 Arkansas Firms Among Top in Fields for Stock Prices," *Arkansas Gazette*, 20 October 1985, sec. D; Rick Telberg, "Food-Service Stock Index Soars 32% Propelled by a Few Top Performers," *Nation's Restaurant News*, 13 January 1986, p. 1ff; "The 400 Richest People in America," *Forbes*, 27 October 1986, p. 294. The primary source of material used in this biography was a telephone interview the authors conducted with Mr. Hickingbotham on 2 December 1986.

Isbell, Marion W.

Jimmy Starr, "History of Ramada Inns, Inc." (a privately published 56-page pamphlet on the origins of the company by its former advertising director, written in 1975). Most of the information used in the preparation of this biography was obtained from a telephone interview the authors conducted with Mr. Isbell on 2 April 1986. A great deal of material also was obtained from Lucy Diana, archivist, Ramada Inns, Inc., Phoenix.

Krieble, Vernon K.

Ellsworth S. Grant, *Drop by Drop* (Newington, CT: privately published corporate history, 1983); "Professor Krieble's Magic Goo,"

Fortune, November 1956, p. 176; "True Grip," *Forbes*, 15 October 1977, p. 136; "Loctite: Ready to Fend Off a Flock of New Competitors," *Business Week*, 19 June 1978, pp. 116 and 118; Arthur M. Louis, "New Rich of the Seventies," September 1973, pp. 170 and 238; Vernon Krieble obituary, *New York Times*, 24 January 1964. The authors conducted a telephone interview with Dr. Krieble's son, Robert Krieble, on 14 January 1986.

LeVine, Bill

John Merwin, "Postal Instant Success," *Forbes*, 2 February 1981, pp. 56 and 59; David C. Lustig, "A PIP of a Franchise," *Entrepreneur*, January 1986, pp. 124–25; "Secrets of Winners: Postal Instant Press," *The Franchise Advisor*, July 1986, pp. 50–51. The authors obtained most of the information used in the preparation of this biography from a telephone interview conducted with Mr. LeVine on 10 October 1986.

Mendel, Perry

Geoffrey Smith, "Perry Mendel's Golden Diapers," *Forbes*, 25 June 1979, pp. 67–69; Joseph Lelyveld, "Drive-In Day Care," *New York Times* Sunday Magazine, 5 June 1977, p. 110; "What Mass-Produced Child Care Is Producing," *Fortune*, 28 November 1983, pp. 157–58ff. Robert Metz, "Life Insurance for Toddlers," *New York Times*, 5 July 1978, sec. IV; "Two Enterprises Worth Nursing," *Fortune*, May 1975, p. 65. The authors conducted a telephone interview with Mr. Mendel on 18 February 1986.

Millard, William H.

Mr. Millard declined repeated requests for interviews, leaving the authors to rely primarily on previously published material. Sources include Robert Levering, Michael Katz, and Milton Moskowitz, *The Computer Entrepreneurs* (New York: New American Library, 1984), s.v. "William Millard"; A. David Silver, *Entrepreneurial Megabucks* (New York: John Wiley & Sons, 1985), s.v. "William Millard"; Michael Brody, "Computerland's Suddenly Poorer Boss," *Fortune*, 15 April 1985, p. 124ff; Kathleen K. Wiegner, "The Instant Billionaire," *Forbes*, 5 December 1983, pp. 39–41; Gene Bylinsky, "The Computer Stores Have Arrived," *Fortune*, 24 April 1978, pp. 52–55; Pauline Yoshihashi, "A Daughter's Quick Rise to the Top," *New York Times*, 16 December 1984, sec. III; Deborah C. Wise, "How To Sell Computers Today—And How Not To," *Business Week*, 2 September 1985, pp. 70 and 72; "ComputerLand Fight Is Developing," *New York Times*,

231

13 March 1985, sec. IV; "The Forbes Four Hundred," *Forbes,* 1 October 1984, pp. 86 and 87. The authors conducted a telephone interview with Normal Dinnsen, one of the earliest ComputerLand franchisees, on 10 November 1986.

Mintz, David

Paul B. Brown, "Mixing Fleishig and Tofutti," *Forbes,* 7 May 1984, p. 82; William E. Geist, "High Hopes for Pushcart Sales of Frozen Tofu," *New York Times,* 20 June 1984, sec. III; "Tofu on the Mind," ibid., 14 September 1984, sec. III. The authors' primary source of material used in the preparation of this biography was a telephone interview with Mr. Mintz conducted on 30 October 1986.

Mullany, David

Steven Levy, "The Wiffle Ball," *Esquire,* August 1983, pp. 83 and 85; Dougald MacDonald, "Wiffle Ball: A 33-Year-Old Toy Is Still Just a 'Kids' Toy' to Its Maker," *New England Business,* 17 February 1986, p. 29; Ric Bucher, "The Gift of Wiffle," *Yankee,* October 1985, pp. 239 and 168–73; Paul B. Brown, "The Road Not Taken," *Forbes,* 8 October 1984, p. 62; Roger Holmes, "Mr. Wiffle," *New England Monthly,* July 1984, pp. 28 and 29. Much of the material used in the preparation of this biography was obtained from two telephone interviews the authors conducted with Mr. Mullany and his son, David A. Mullany, Jr., on 9 March 1986.

Norman, David A.

The most complete published source of information on Mr. Norman and Businessland is the 2 December 1985 issue of *Computer + Software News,* virtually all of which is devoted to the company. Other sources include Tom Quinlan, "1985 Is a Year of Vindication for Businessland's David Norman," *Computer Retail News,* 18 November 1985, pp. 149 and 200; Deborah C. Wise, "How To Sell Computers Today—And How Not To," *Business Week,* 2 September 1985, pp. 70 and 72; Robert Scott, "Businessland Plans $30 Million Convertible Debenture Offering," *Computer + Software News,* 27 January 1986, p. 16; "Silicon Isn't all There Is in Silicon Valley," *San Jose Mercury News,* 20 January 1986, sec. C. The authors conducted a telephone interview with Mr. Norman on 23 April 1986.

Norman, Merle N.

Connie O'Kelley, *Merle Nethercutt Norman: An American Success Story* (Los Angeles: privately published, 1976); Robert Levering, Milton

Moskowitz, and Michael Katz, *The 100 Best Companies to Work For* (Reading, MA: Addison-Wesley Co., 1984), s.v. "Merle Norman Cosmetics"; Ellen Paris, "Age Before Beauty," *Forbes,* 9 September 1985, pp. 78 and 80. The authors conducted a telephone interview with Ms. Norman's nephew, J. B. Nethercutt, on 24 March 1986.

Norris, William C.

Katherine Davis Fishman, *The Computer Establishment* (New York: McGraw Hill Book Co., 1981, s.v. "Control Data"; Carol Pine and Susan Mundale, *Self-Made: The Stories of Twelve Minnesota Entrepreneurs* (Minneapolis: Dorn Books, 1982), s.v. "William Norris"; Gregory H. Wierzynski, "Control Data's Newest Cliffhanger," *Fortune,* February 1968, pp. 126–29ff; Eric N. Berg, "Control Data's Fall From Grace," *New York Times,* 17 February 1985, sec III; "Control Data Starts a Painful Retrenchment," *Business Week,* 22 October 1984, pp. 94 and 96; "Control Data: Is There Room for Change After Bill Norris?," ibid., 17 October 1983, p. 119ff; Michael W. Fedo, "How Control Data Turns a Profit on Its Good Works," *New York Times,* 7 January 1979, sec. III; Ernest Holsendolph, "Control Data Seeks Broad Base," ibid., 16 January 1973, pp. 51 and 57; David Finn, "A Computer Pioneer's Deals and Ideals," *Across the Board,* April 1986, pp. 20–28; Patrick Houston, "Control Data's Struggle to Come Back From the Brink," *Business Week,* 14 October 1985, pp. 62 and 63. The authors conducted a telephone interview with Mr. Norris on 6 March 1986.

Paxson, Lowell W., and Speer, Roy M.

Mr. Paxson and Mr. Speer declined to be interviewed, leaving the authors to rely on secondary sources. Among those sources were Peter J. Boyer, "Going to the Mall on Cable TV," *New York Times,* 13 June 1986, sec. D; James Cox, "Airing Deals for Armchair Shoppers," *USA Today,* 7 August 1986, sec. B; Michael Winerip, "TV Shopping Brings the Mall to the Home," *New York Times,* 27 April 1986, sec. I; Bonnie Welch, "A Shopaholic's TV Paradise Goes Public," *Florida Trend,* June 1986, pp. 65–68; Tim Allis and Linda Marx, "Cable's Home Shopping Network Holds This Truth to Be Self-Evident—No American Should Pay Retail," *People Weekly,* 11 August 1986, p. 107ff; Richard H. Stewart, "The TV Yard Sale," *Boston Sunday Globe,* 2 February 1986, pp. 14 and 16; James Cox, "TV's Discount Hawkers Losing Millions," *USA Today,* 19 February 1987, sec. A; Fonda Anderson, "Home Shopping Network Sells Products, Flash in Clearwater," *Tampa Bay Business,* 23–29 March 1986, p. 1ff; Dale

Kasler, "Merchandise Is the Message," *Tampa Tribune,* 8 June 1986, sec. E; "Big Gamble for Home Shopping," *Dun's Business Month,* September 1986, p. 21; "The Four Hundred Richest People in America," *Forbes,* 27 October 1986, p. 168. Additional material was provided by Judy Luden, Home Shopping Network, Clearwater, Florida.

Plumly, George W.

Marion Buckley, "Showing People the Door," *Texas Business,* November 1985, pp. 87–88; Julius Karash, "Inventor Creates Safety Lighting for Airline Use," *Fort Worth Star-Telegram,* Accent Section, pp. 1–2; John A. Byrne, "It Ain't Over Until It's Over," *Forbes,* 15 July 1985, p. 104; Stewart Swartz, "FAA Approves First Floor-Proximity Lighting System," *Airline Executive,* October 1985, p. 37; "Floor-Proximity Emergency Lighting System," *Avionics,* March 1986, p. 27; "FAA Approves Escape Lighting System for Aircraft," *Aviation Daily,* 10 September 1985, p. 44. Most of the material used in the preparation of this biography was obtained from a telephone interview the authors conducted with Mr. Plumly on 22 May 1986.

Psarouthakis, John

Ray Slelp, "Revitalizing Sick Companies Is His Specialty," *Ann Arbor News,* 31 July 1983, pp. 16 and 17; George White, "Executive Enjoys Well-Calculated Risks," *Detroit Free Press,* 11 August 1986, sec. E; "John Psarouthakis: Whipping Underdog Companies Into Shape," *Business Week,* 11 August 1986, p. 74; "JP Industries' Unglamorous Growth," *Ann Arbor Observer,* September 1985, p. 23ff. Most of the material used in the preparation of this biography was obtained from a personal interview the authors conducted with Dr. Psarouthakis on 18 November 1986.

Roach, Alfred J.

John A. Byrne, "Up From Harlem," *Forbes,* 21 November 1983, pp. 56 and 58; Fred Bratman, "A Lesson From Nuns May Pay Off in China," *New York Times,* 4 November 1979, sec. XX1; "Bell Ringer," *Barron's,* 13 February 1984, p. 50; "What Happens When," *Corporate Public Issues,* 15 March 1982, p. 1; "Congress Urged to Fight Japanese 'Takeover'," *San Juan Star,* 7 February 1982, sec. B; Harry L. Fridman, "TII's Twin-Plant Plan Produces Big Job Gain," ibid., 12 May 1985, sec. B; Leonard Sloane, "Insurgents Win Brewer Control," *New York Times,* 22 May 1965, sec. I; "New Biotechnology Venture Based on Campus," *University of Notre Dame President's Newsletter,* January 1985, p. 3. The authors obtained most of the information used in the preparation of this article from a telephone interview conducted with Mr. Roach on 3 April 1986.

Rossi, Anthony T.

Arthur M. Louis, "Tony Rossi Can't Let Go," *Fortune,* 16 January 1978, pp. 120–21ff; Wayne King, "A Taste for Profits," *New York Times,* 16 June 1974, sec. III; Irvin S. Taubkin, "Tropicana Busily Expanding Citrus Domain," ibid., 16 June 1972, pp. 53 and 62; Arthur M. Louis, "The New Rich of the Seventies," *Fortune,* September 1973, p. 242; "The Would-Be Explorer Who Started Tropicana," *New York Times,* 16 January 1979, sec. IV; Robert J. Cole, "Beatrice, Tropicana in Merger," ibid., 8 August 1978, sec. IV. The authors conducted an interview with Mr. Rossi through the mail in the spring of 1986 and a telephone interview with his close friend and associate, Ed H. Price, on 23 June 1986.

Sarno, Sam A.

Debra Skodack, "Coupons Clip Cost for Consumers," *El Paso Herald-Post,* 18 June 1984, sec. B; Robert H. Bork, "Getting Rich on Cents-Off Coupons," *Forbes,* 16 January 1984, pp. 59 and 62; Mary Ann Linsen, "High-Flying Coupons Soar to the Skies," *Progressive Grocer,* February 1981, p. 65ff. Most of the material used in the preparation of this biography was obtained from a telephone interview the authors conducted with Mr. Sarno on 24 April 1986.

Schneider, Ralph E.

Editors of the *Wall Street Journal, The New Millionaires and How They Made It* (New York: Bernard Geis Associates, 1960), pp. 92–102; "Credit Cards for Anything? "*Newsweek,* 28 July 1958, pp. 68–69ff; "Diners Club Scouts New Fields," *Business Week,* 21 November 1959, pp. 68–70 and 74; Horace Sutton, "Is Cash Obsolete?," *Saturday Review,* 18 October 1958, pp. 40–41; Irwin Ross, "The Credit Card's Painful Coming of Age," *Fortune,* October 1971, pp. 108–11ff; "On-the-Cuff Travel Speeds Up," *Business Week,* 16 August 1958, p. 111; "Credit Card 'Pays' Entertainment Bills," ibid., 11 November 1950, p. 34; Charge It Please," *Time,* 9 April 1951, p. 100; "Credit Card Game," ibid., 22 September 1958, pp. 82 and 84; "Dining on the Cuff," *Newsweek,* 29 January 1951, p. 73; "Tougher Going for Credit Cards," *Business Week,* 10 September 1960, p. 49; "Credit Cards Stir Up Rebellion," ibid., 21 March 1959, p. 36; "Factor Acquired by Diners Club," *New York Times,* 6 June 1961, sec. I; "Diners Club Eyes Deal with a Rival," ibid., 11 November 1961, sec. I; "Diners Club is

Buying Electronic Imprinters," ibid., 14 May 1961, sec. III; Ralph Schneider obituary, *New York Times,* 3 November 1964, sec. I; and Frank X. McNamara obituary, ibid., 11 November 1957, sec. I. The authors conducted a telephone interview with Mr. Schneider's son, Robert Schneider, on 25 February 1986.

Sontheimer, Carl G.

Anne Anable, "Miracle in the Kitchen, a Fortune in the Bank," *New York Times,* 16 April 1978, sec. XXIII; "You've Got to Blow Your Horn," *Forbes,* 4 February 1980, pp. 94–95; Stacy V. Jones, "Electric Eye Spurns Bogus Bills, Another Invention Aids Puzzlers," *New York Times,* 21 January 1956, pp. 27 and 30. Most of the material used in the preparation of this biography was obtained from a telephone interview that the authors conducted with Mr. Sontheimer on 20 April 1986.

Tushinsky, Joseph S.

Pamela G. Hollie, "Well Past 65, They're Still Boss," *New York Times,* 29 July 1979, sec. III; "Get Yourself a Geisha," *Forbes,* 15 November 1973, p. 126; Thomas M. Pryor, "New Scope Added to Standard Film," *New York Times,* 7 March 1954, sec. I; Bosley Crowther, "The Screen in Review," ibid., 24 March 1954, sec. I; "Guarnieri's Last Session," *Musical Merchandise Review,* November 1985, p. 72. Most of the information used in the preparation of this biography was obtained from a telephone interview the authors conducted with Mr. Tushinsky on 10 February 1986.

Index